ONE-SENTENCE STORIES

Intriguing New Anthology Of Stories Told in a Single Sentence

Written by
Amazing Authors
Compiled and Barely Edited by
Val Dumond
Muddy Puddle Press

BOOK#2 One-Sentence Stories
© 2018 Muddy Puddle Press
All rights reserved. No part of this book may be copied or reproduced in any form without the written permission of Muddy Puddle Press, with the exception of reproductions allowed by the authors, who maintain possession of all rights to their own work.

ISBN: 978-0-9985489-2-0

Printed in the United States of America

Muddy Puddle Press
P O Box 97124
Lakewood WA 98497

Cover created by Strange Design (strangedesigndk@outlook.com)

Gertrude Stein

(1874-1946)

"You will write if you will write without thinking of the result in terms of a result, but think of the writing in terms of discovery, which is to say that creation must take place between the pen and the paper, not before in a thought or afterwards in a recasting... (for) it will come if it is there and if you will let it come." (66 words)

—Gertrude Stein

Contents

Ain't We Got Fun!	vii
Lushootseed Names Remain	1
My Best Worst-Movie Review	2
Elder Eyeballing at Starbucks	3
off	4
A Run-On Life	5
Why Use Ten Words When 200 Will Do?	6
Murder! Or Not?	7
Lights Out	8
Peter, Peter, Pumpkin Eater	9
When Loreen Thinks Back to Meeting Buck…	10
Thrift Store Guitar Grace-Song	11
The Spool Table	12
Remembering Friends	13
Musings	14
Try It, You'll Like It	15
Third-Eye Strength	16
Loreen and Buck Play the Video Game…	17
Walking into Darkness	19
A Perfect Sunday Afternoon	20
Cinnamon Bear	22
When Will We Stop Pretending?	24
Watermelon	26
Swallowing	28
Deferred Judgment	30
This Is Who I Am	32
I'm Still Here at 85	34
Are You Hungary?	38
January	40
Martin	42
A Cautionary Tale	44
Hey!	46

The Night the Doodlebug Hit 48
Carbon Forest: 50
Delay 52
Delicate Balance 54
Enough for Merle and Me 56
We Were on the Same Page 58
There Are Cars; Then There Are CARS 60
A Consequence of De-cluttering 62
Why Do I Speak Spanish in Public? 64
Rosalia 66
My Mother the Trekkie 68
Oh What a Brute-of-a Morning! 70
My Real-life Miracle! 72
Like He Didn't Know… 76
The Easy Choices 78
pocket-sized scythe 80
Alley People 82
Lida Rose 85
My Careers 88
Bruce the Plumber 91
Me Too, Gotcha! 94
Lookie, Cookie 97
Quiet Time 100
It's Heart Surgery for Goodness Sake 103
Karmic Fishing Trip 106
New Beginnings…Again 109
Distractions in a Suitcase 113
Escape the Dark 117
The Drugstore on the Corner 121
Fateful Flight Suit 125
My New Computer Toy 130
Pulling on a Thread 135
About the Authors 141

Ain't We Got Fun!

WHAT THE HECK, YOU MAY ASK, is a one-sentence story? A good definition: a story told in a single sentence. It could be a short, very short sentence or it could be a long, very long sentence. For the purpose of this anthology, the specified number of words is between 200 and 2000. "Any sentence can be made longer…" according to Professor Steven Pinker, Ph.D.

And that's what started this idea of constructing a long sentence that tells a story. Never mind what Teacher warned about "run-on" sentences! Never mind what writing professors tell you. Just put your pen to paper or fingers to computer and W-R-I-T-E!

As for merits? That's up to the writer — anyone who writes, whether for business or for telling fictitious stories for fun. We write to inform, question, describe, document (relate what happened), and to express our souls.

You hear it all the time. "They do it with movies; they do it with television shows; they do it with jazz music; and they even do it on Broadway!" *They* believe that when the first — the original — presentation is well received, it's time to produce another one.

This book is the second presentation of *One-Sentence Stories*, starring many of the original cast of writers who wrote noticeably longer new stories this time, and also starring many new writers who have added new and exciting stories. The fun doesn't stop!

One-sentence story writing originated with a challenge from the noted Dr. Steven Pinker, MIT professor, linguist, and author of such books as *The Language Instinct* and *The Sense of*

Style. In both books, he cited long sentences in literature with "as many as 340 words", adding "every sentence can be made longer". Well, what writer can ignore such a challenge! That's when the fun began.

Writers soon came up with their own extraordinary ways of writing a sentence. In this book you'll discover how Benjamin Lukoff uses the International Phonetic Alphabet-derived Lushootseed alphabet to represent native place names. And how holly woodie eschews capital letters and punctuation altogether — and both express intriguing stories in unique styles, as do all these 44 fabulous writers.

Writers now report that this *word-doodling* has been going on for some time, and whether you call it *word-doodling, playing with words, sentence-stretching,* or *silly sentences,* it has its advantages.

One of them is reducing stress; who can't use that? Another is re-focusing, as in what to do when a writer hits that well-known writer's block. Still another advantage is emptying the mind of story words that have congregated in the head and need expelling. But the fun comes with the realization that you're writing those much-maligned "run-on sentences" that Teacher warned about back in grammar school. We salute you, English teachers (some of whom contributed to *BOOK#2*) for — ironically — using one-sentence writing to teach ways to use various parts of the English language.

Now therapists working with patients under mental stress are using the project in a different way. When they encouraged patients to write down their dreams, they discovered the lack of punctuation, which often made clear the brain's confusion. Don't be surprised if a new book comes out with a title like *One-Sentence Stories for Dreamers.*

But wait! There's more! Writers can use one-sentence writing to develop an idea into a story, or take apart a story by separating the scenes.

Yes, the one-sentence story offers potential to *all* people who write. Have you ever sat in a dull meeting and wished you were on a beach somewhere? Use your pen (look as if you're taking notes) and write how you would feel on that beach. You'll walk out of that meeting with a smile on your face and a good story in your briefcase. It's also good medicine to ease your mind while waiting for a dentist's appointment, or in the midst of a day wrangling children, or anxious over an upcoming exam, or just plain weary of daily problems....

For sheer fun — the run-away-and-forget-daily-woes kind of fun — you won't find an easier activity than word-doodling a one-sentence story. Write it; stow it away in a file; and when the file is full, publish *Your Collection of One-Sentence Stories*. This book is brought to you by Muddy Puddle Press, P O Box 97124, Lakewood WA 98497, and muddypuddle@live.com.

—Val Dumond

Muddy Puddle Press

[*The stories in this book are arranged according to the number of words, indicated at the end of each story, all the way from 203-1989. And please note that most of the stories can be extended even longer! Find information about the authors at the back of the book.*]

x / Book#2 One-Sentence Stories

Lushootseed Names Remain
by Benjamin Lukoff

Before white settlers came to *dzidzəlalič* in 1852, before they came to *sčəgʷaliču* in 1832, even before they first sighted the shores of *xʷəlč* in 1792, the *dxʷdəwʔabš* were here, living at *sluʔwił* and *šilšul, babaqʷəb* and *t'uʔalalʔtxʷ*, and *paq'ác'ałčuʔ* and *səxʷt'ičib*, by the lakes called *c'alq'ʷadiʔ* and *sisałtəb* and *dxʷƛ'əš* and *xáxəʔčuʔ*, and most of all *xačuʔ* — the lake — the smaller ones being fed by springs like *liq'təd* where the waters run red, *the* lake being fed by the river whose mouth was at *ƛ'axʷadis*, but one by one their names were replaced by the settlers, who though they named the city for *siʔał* and the river for the *dxʷdəwʔabš* nevertheless named places Pioneer Square for themselves, or Fremont for where they came from, or Brooklyn for that which they aspired to be, and while *šilšul* became Shilshole and *liq'təd* became Licton, other *dxʷləšúcid* names were left unwritten and hardly spoken for decades but still remembered — so let Carkeek remain Carkeek, but know that it was once and is still *kʷaatəb*, as Montlake is still *staxʷugʷił*, the Locks, which lowered *xačuʔ* and *xáxəʔčuʔ*, still *xʷiwálqʷ*, and University Village still *sluʔwił* village, and celebrate that *wətəbʔaltxʷ* now sits where Whitman and Stevens meet. (203)

My Best Worst-Movie Review
by Richard Silverman

AS AN INVETERATE CINEPHILE with some free time on my hands, I couldn't resist the temptation to see the new Hollywood film, "The Disaster Artist", produced and directed by James Franco and costarring his less famous, but arguably more handsome brother, David Franco… a barely believable but true story about the making of a low budget independent 2003 film titled, "The Room" (they say the acting is consistently cringe worthy), which was produced, written, and directed by Tommy Wiseau, a heretofore unknown filmmaker with an extremely annoying unidentifiable accent who is unabashedly proud that his movie has become infamously known as the worst movie ever made, even though after a few years of invisibility, critical disdain, and financial failure, it eventually became a late-night cult classic and modest box office success even before the Franco brothers and several other famous actors (like Seth Rogen, Melanie Griffith, and Sharon Stone, among others) inspired it to become the recently renowned disaster plot of a 2018 Golden Globe Award that I can't deny is quite engaging, strangely funny, and totally unlike any film I've ever seen, yet paradoxically a well-done cinematic creation about a god-awful movie that I find myself oddly (dare I say perversely) very eager to see. (206)

Elder Eyeballing at Starbucks
by Richard Silverman

WHILE MY LIFE HAS CHANGED dramatically as an aging-but-healthy septuagenarian, there are a few things that remain constant and very pleasurable for me to this day: drinking good coffee, reading and watching videos on my IPad, creative writing and observing beautiful females of all shapes, sizes, races and ages wherever I go… like the tall, bouncy, 40-ish blonde that sauntered through the Starbucks entrance last Saturday morning with a most striking upbeat rhythm tapping away from her shiny apple-red high-heels, which seemed to be evoking an unselfconscious "I'm so sexy" drumming as she passed my table, smiling back at me with wide-open, glistening eyes and an unabashed very-happy-to see-you grin, as if she were enjoying our spontaneous hetero-chemistry almost as much as I was savoring it, being the ever-romantic man I've always been… yes, losing myself in my ageless *mantasy*, reminding myself that although some of my male vitality has definitely waned in recent years and I've not had a real-life lover for almost a decade, my aroused geezer pupils still dilate at the sight of female beauty, especially when the woman responds like I remember Wendy's wet eyes gazing at me as we fell into bed together, anticipating the easily delicious entwining our bodies always merged into from the very first time we embraced unadorned. (216)

off
by holly woodie

universes of thoughtful thought radiate off the ceilings and walls where the tempest is finally caught beginning again whenever we open the book entitled where have you been and what ought you have been doing when all around war stampedes on inside outside with the global befallen in spaces occupied by purest hatred taught by parents and guardians at backyard barbeque get-togethers raising hate in forward places like schools parks mosques and churches when all we want is to learn to play or worship in peaceful spaces until streets and blocks are blockaded and made to suffer worse than death and made to take part even in disagreement reminiscing in disgust apart from the crowd by heavy choice and we bow out for the valleys and mountains where what we build is built by hand and what we grow is ours to share living life off the grid of hatred doing our part by calling and writing legislators and attending protests to help us see through the laden masses caked in lies betrayal and dirt and try as we might nothing budges not even our car with a damn blowout on our way to the once capital for the protest of the century where the new pea ohh tee eeyew sss has tweeted his hate every day since he took the high seat (223)

A Run-On Life
by Nick Page

UNLIKE A RUN-ON SENTENCE, unlike a winged chariot, unlike a deceitful wind, unlike language, easy words, thoughts unfolding, unlike a silent choir praying for breath, praying for the sacred, unlike a baby reciting Shakespeare with her eyes, conducting Bach with her precious fingers, unlike jealous water, earth, the filth of promise in rich soil, unlike the morning, she dreams of unknown things, unseen things, her hair dances in run-on illusions, the so-called reality of things unreal, and she inhabits her dream like the loon in the night, like the rose rising from rich soil, like humble raindrops envious of the mighty seas, like the precious fingers of a child dancing to the music of exploding stars, the giggling babe, "If you tickle us, do we not laugh?", like the time time time in the breath between one melody and the next, like ripples of thought, like words, like wind unconcerned with what is truth and what is lies, like a run-on sentence, she is powerless to fight her dream, riding its winged chariot, waking to that which is real, chastising herself for her inability to fight her dreams, an audience to her own mind, and wondering of this so-called reality, this real world of this and that and time and morning, night, and wondering if she should question the run-on sentence of her life. (224)

Why Use Ten Words When 200 Will Do?
by Jeff Laskowski

AFTER A FEW SECONDS OF SEARCHING in the dark, my wandering fingers finally found and firmly pressed down on the small protruding alarm button to silence the shrill and bothersome buzzer on the vintage faux-wood-grain clock radio, a purchase carefully selected at a nearby thrift store, I eventually summoned up enough inertia to rise up while at the same time I swung my weary 60-year-old legs sideways from underneath the mismatched sheet and blanket to slowly slither down the side of the bed, and as my feet made contact with the slightly worn carpet-covered floor, I rubbed the sleep out of my sand-dusted eyes and reached for my sleek new smartphone to see what the weather was going to be like outside this morning so I could appropriately select the color-coordinated high-tech bicycling apparel that would cover my svelte and toned body for the ten-mile-plus commute on my silver forty-five-year-old Sears Free Spirit two-wheeler over the well-traveled asphalt thoroughfare to the private, not-so-local, sport and racquet club where I was scheduled to meet with three of my not-so-friendly combatants and take to the court for an arduous hour and fifteen minutes of physical battle over three sets of tennis, often punctuated with trash-talking, to see who would have bragging rights until the next time we would meet, in other words (just 10): I arose today and went to play tennis with friends! (232)

Murder! Or Not?
by Kate McPhail

HE WAS DEAD, OR AT LEAST HE THOUGHT he was dead as he couldn't feel his left leg (to be honest, maybe his left leg was dead while the rest of him was still alive) but as his brain still worked, less well than usual to be honest, he decided that he was probably only half dead, so began to take an inventory to see how much dead — or not-dead — he actually was and he started at his left leg because he already knew that was dead (after all, if it was alive, he should feel it, or at least its presence) and worked his way from there to the right leg, which seemed twisted at an odd angle, but otherwise alive, as were both of his arms, which he was troubled to find were cold and maybe slightly wet and his heart jumped as he wondered if the dampness of blood felt different than the dampness of rain or river water or whatever was making his arms wet, but as he continued upwards, he discovered that everything seemed to be in working- or thinking-order and so decided that maybe his body, except for his obviously dead left leg, was, after all, alive and not dead and only then, did he realize that he was lying on the ground where he had fallen after slipping on an icy patch of snow. (295)

Lights Out
by Susan de la Vergne

On a stormy Monday morning at a meeting about impending layoffs, a perky HR rep and three dour executives (more worried than usual about the company's bottom line) sat around a conference table, watched the lights flicker, stay on, flicker again, then go out, and though the HR rep remained cheerful, the execs shared knowing glances in the half-darkness as they realized that it would take more than a single round of layoffs to save their company from bankruptcy, which they all knew was the company's fate, though they continued to try various strategies and tactics to save it, knowing all along in the backs of their minds that it was probably hopeless, and now they were about to resort to an overused and under-inspired idea — reducing expenses by laying off people — which every desperate company does even though their leadership teams know it rarely solves anything, but there they were, these three dour execs and the perky HR rep, about to summarily dismiss people from jobs they liked and did well, a last-ditch effort that was the execs' very last idea, in which they had little confidence, but they knew that when the lights came on, if the lights came on, they'd be letting people go, cutting staff size almost in half before 5:00 p.m., a gruesome prospect which was really just a stopgap measure and which they all knew would lead them not out of trouble but deeper into it. (242)

Peter, Peter, Pumpkin Eater
by Jane Lang

THIS IS AN OLD STORY and for the sake of argument just pretend you had a wife who spent money like a Vanderbilt and did not know her place (once the place had been established), as in the case of Peter and his wife, who for the sake of clarity we will call Clarice, a shopaholic who loved to cruise the malls, always recognizing a sale, with a nose for a bargain and sexy underwire bras, a tantalizing little minx, and as I was saying, unfortunately she did not know her place — and here I admit the situation could have been uncomfortable for Clarice and more than likely a little embarrassing — to find herself in a pumpkin shell, and while Clarice was not one easily embarrassed, she found it to be quite awkward, but I am sure you know what I mean, so she decided to defy Peter and one way or another become a liberated woman because we all realize how difficult it must be to maintain a loving relationship if one party is living with his head in the clouds and can't see the pumpkins for all the corn stalks in the rows around them, and because Clarice was high-strung and very high-maintenance and supposed to be at home (in the pumpkin shell), when all she wanted was to display her independence and extraordinary good taste in lingerie, so she did the only thing she could and fled, finding hers an untenable situation, leaving Peter with his pumpkin shell (empty by the way), but still thinking he was keeping her very well. (264)

When Loreen Thinks Back to Meeting Buck…
by Nita Penfold

She remembers having dinner at Dottie's with a retired Marine pretty-boy that Dottie met by dialing the wrong number, something they joked about only their teenage children doing, but Dottie figures it's safe to have him over with Loreen and all the children there since he's a Vietnam Vet, a battered women's advocate, a closet Libertarian from a large working-class family, has had three wives, two daughters, one stepson, a granddaughter, and works with his hands fixing copiers but studies nights so he can be a lawyer, and Loreen remembers thinking he could charm a swarm of bees from their hive, then convince them it was his idea all along, and she's intrigued by his laugh, his wit, the commitment he holds to the custody of his daughter, how he went out at midnight to find another birthday cake for her when she cried because no piece was saved as promised for her best friend, and the kind of man who carries crayons in his car, and Loreen thinks Dottie is crazy for not wanting to date him while she herself has clearly been dating the wrong type of man — way too many never-married androgynous new-age men who want to explore their feminine sides by painting amorphous water color shapes or learning to folk-dance or make bread, instead of actually committing to another human being by tapping deep within themselves to find their own nurturing side — then three days later, Buck asks Dottie for Loreen's phone number and Loreen okays it because, for a change, she wants to date a man who knows he's a man instead of a wannabe. (271)

Thrift Store Guitar Grace-Song
by Panjah of Jesus

I GREW UP IN A HOUSE FULL of mother's chosen religion where the rules were the standards and the stairs led up to heaven, and no matter how many steps I took towards those stairs on any given day, I would always end up in square one the next day because those steps were faulty and rickety and full of fraudulent traps meant to ensnare my young soul in a never-ending search for perfection through good works and the keeping of the law, something impossible for a sin-soaked sinner like me to do and therefore, meant to keep me in a cyclical hamster-wheel trap as if trying to strike a deal with God for my eternal soul, something so tiring, I know, but I had no choice because this opioid of the masses was incense in my nose since I was a child and I inhaled its putrid perfume instead of mother's scent through hugs, and therefore was nearly asphyxiated through it by age sixteen when the cult's board of elders expelled me from their heavy oak doors into the pagan world full of demons, sins, and Armageddon, things they had hammered into my impressionable imagination from the pulpit, so as to teach me, a black sheep found kissing boys, a lesson, a very traumatic event that catapulted me into a restless search for the true God full of love and not hate, who I found in a desert where I played my thrift-store guitar and asked for another chance, and He came and showed me grace in the beautiful face of Christ Jesus, and I was healed and I was saved, yes and amen. (275)

The Spool Table
by Carol Wissmann

WE LAUGHED TOGETHER, recapturing memories shared from living through the same era, until I announced, "I still have it here in the den doing duty as a desk for the telephone," and as the physical distance between her and me diminished, tied together as we were by the telephone lines, time turned backward as I contemplated where the ubiquitous spools originated, since every self-respecting "hippie" had one because they were utilitarian, coming in all sizes, perhaps reels spanning the miles of cable that now linked us, industrial bobbins that when turned on their sides served as everything from kitchen tables to bedsteads — so when she blurted out, "I remember it!" as her recollection mingled with mine, I shared that I'd even painted mine barn-red, my attempt at interior design that left us giggling, when I added "Oh, and for years I kept that millefiore candle on it", the candle of a thousand flowers, the most beautiful in my collection of many, coupled with the spool table (no hippie-home would be complete without candles, lots of candles lighting cost-cutting nights to keep electricity at a minimum), and then she interjected in a voice that sent the phone lines vibrating, "Oh my God," which she fairly screamed, "I remember the candle too!" and as we talked on, reminiscing, the spool once again rolled easily between the two of us, though occasionally, our times together had tangled, like chain snagged, caught in twists and knots, but on that night on the telephone, the thread between us unraveled as easily as a ball of dropped yarn, and now that line strung from some long-ago spool connected the lives of two old friends. (279)

Remembering Friends
by Paul T. Jackson

THE OTHER DAY I WAS READING some notes and someone asked about a particular song, and I suggested they check the book *Only a Miner* that was produced back in the late 1960s by my friend and colleague, Archie Green, with whom we shared a ride one year from Columbus, Ohio, to New York City, along with my first wife, and that got me to thinking again about our relationship, and on searching I found someone had indeed written a Wikipedia article about him and as well, more recently, a biography entitled simply *Archie Green* that has to be, to me anyway, a wonderful gift to his memory and for anyone who knew him since he wasn't someone who was a notoriously rich celebrity (having worked as a millwright, and professor, folklorist) just someone walking around with the rest of us doing what he loved and with a passion for history of unionism and folksong which, when faced with death you wonder if you are just that kind of person who just walks around with the rest of us, but are indeed the celebrity that others will count when you are gone with your contributions to others great enough to be valued by many and documented, the reason many of us collect papers, such as receipts, letters, greeting cards, proposals, peripheral writings, news clippings, et al, so that when we are gone we can be counted, valued and documented, that we counted and our life was significant to others, that our life made a difference to another and brings sweet memories to those who knew us and beyond and we can, in our ether of non-existence, say, "Wow, I did good." (281)

Musings
by Paul T. Jackson

It's time I write something of a story because it's time to write a one-sentence story, which usually are musings about various things that happen when there are no other things to do, that leads me to fully wonder why so many people get confused about libraries when the American Library Association is so big and provides an umbrella, well not totally, but the ALA is confused with other such library associations as the Public Library Association, the College and Research Library Association, and other independent groups such as the Special Libraries Association, Church and Synagogue Library Association (oops, that one has been disbanded) for diversity of the denominations' library associations and regional church libraries groups, while all the time a given librarian might have to join several of the associations because now the diversity requires one to have a good, wider knowledge of all the knowledge groups, as if knowledge management and information overload groups don't have enough to do with just one organization, and it seems like all librarians now have to be specialists similar to doctors — who even within one profession such as cancer treatment where a patient like myself ends up with seven doctors and various physician's assistants, and nurses scattered among five distinct organizations within the umbrella group "CHI Franciscan Health and Cancer Group" — so that librarians must become specialists too, much like music, theatre, performing arts associations and all so that at some point it becomes a gig society whereby librarian specialists will start visiting different libraries as their gig, so a patron will have to wait to get their questions answered on a given day when the doctor … er … the librarian is in. (282)

Try It, You'll Like It!
by Marsha Willsey

YET ANOTHER DREADED SOCIAL dining situation finds me cringing, eyes darting anywhere but the table where the smiling, smirking waiter places a selection of *delectable* appetizers for all to enjoy and though I ever so politely decline, I hear the strident call of "Try it, you'll like it!" from one of our party, the cry soon taken up by another, then another of the smug diners as they pop atrocious tidbits into their mouths and once again I ponder why people feel the need to push their dining perversions on others and why I would feel an obligation to accept their insistent challenge, knowing as I do that no matter how obliging, though long-suffering I be, their hopes will be dashed and their opinion of me confirmed as a culinary wimp with no adventure in my taste buds and I will feel, once again, the unwarranted guilt and see the undeserved disappointment in their eyes — yes *underserved* — as I *have* subjected my unsuspecting palate on more than one occasion (prompted by the haunting refrain of my mother during childhood "we always try in this family") to the horrendous, full body shuddering nastiness of said delicacies, such as the texture deficient calamari, which has the consistency and flavor of a rubber band, the raw oysters that even when drenched in a pot of garlic butter and swallowed as quickly as possible, I swear I can feel their little foot kicking all the way down my throat, and the sushi… so don't even start with the "you don't have to eat raw fish, try the California Roll", yeah, with the yummy seaweed wrapping… because I say "no more!", and I mean, come on people, who do I look like… Mikey? (288)

Third-Eye Strength
by Panjah of Jesus

I WAS AT A TENDER AGE AND NAPPING on the living room couch when I felt something on my forehead as if something was really close to it, and if my forehead had hairs they would all be standing up straight and on point through trails of goosebumps, and since my eyes were half-open, half-closed as they sometimes were when I napped, I could tell it was not a visible object that threatened my forehead's proximity, but the density of the room closing in on me, and I saw the living room as if it were breathing, inching towards me, trying to absorb itself into the center of my forehead, all the while my forehead tried to keep the room at bay, pushed out, resisting the weight, and pushed out like a Wi-Fi signal becoming stronger and stronger, as if lifting weights with an invisible force streaming forth my third eye, as they say, and I always wondered what that meant, what that could have been, but now I know it was my subconscious awareness of my strong and tangible connection to a Living God, a strong yet fragile connection in me from birth, but which the influences of this world slowly somehow sought to cut me off from this pure source of love and joy and light through the traumatic events of molestation, domestic abuse, hurtful words from friends and teachers, rape, drugs, and alcohol, and now that I am older and wiser and can think about this event from an objective point of view, because I now know He has always been there, that I just lost Him from view for a little while until He came and wiped off the debris over my forehead and reconnected my life to His. (293)

Loreen and Buck Play the Video Game...
by Nita Penfold

LETHAL ENFORCERS IS A GAME where players are the police trying to shoot the bank robbers and not their hostages with this plastic gun that you have to tip up to reload — and Buck picks them off one by one in the most difficult and fastest mode of the game, explaining to Loreen the difference between pistols, muskets, chamber revolvers, and automatic weapons with clip magazines, referring to his gun collection in the basement vault, telling her how to make a silencer from a soda can, which drew Loreen to remember asking Buck when they first met how many people he had actually killed in Vietnam, to which Buck had countered by asking her if this was something that would affect the future of their relationship, but Loreen said no, that she was just curious and Buck admitted that he'd had 62 acquired targets confirmed, earning him the Navy Cross, two Silver Stars, two Bronze Stars, a Marine Discretionary Award, and a Lifesaving Medal from the Coast Guard, medals he talks about but she has never seen, and that when he was nineteen, scouting with his recon unit, he had climbed a tree to get a better look when a Vietcong colonel came out into the field and the unit thought they were spotted, but the man was only taking a shit, so Buck carefully shot him in the ass so that he'd always remember Buck when he took a crap — all the while Loreen's shoulders were aching from the intensity of trying to aim at the fast-moving figures when she's only in the easy mode of the game, but she has to admit there is an appeal here, some sense of satisfaction when she blows away the masked figures, but her problem is she keeps killing the bank manager in his suit and tie because he looks like a creep to Loreen. (313)

Walking into Darkness
by Babz Clough

THE WALK KYLIE AND ANGIE TOOK almost every afternoon diverged at Kenmore Square where she gave Kylie a big hug to reassure them both she'd be okay for the next few hours and continued the long walk to her empty apartment as she thought about tomorrow and tomorrow and tomorrow creeping in this petty pace, and she told herself that tomorrow she could get high if she wanted to, she could go buy that little bag of dope, or even better than her buying it, she could call John who haunted her days and nights anyway, and they could get high together sitting in her apartment and liquefying those little square plastic bags of heroin, and she could slide the needle down between her toes so that nobody would ever be able to see the marks, and then, maybe then the pain would stop and she might even feel good because she knew that John would know where to get the good stuff because he was the good stuff, tall and handsome and blue eyed, but still someone who would know where to get a good shot, even if he was good looking and charming and gregarious, as if because he was a drug addict he couldn't be all those other things, too, but maybe they could get high together and maybe they could be happy together because isn't that why people did drugs, because it made them feel better and stronger and she might even find that special place where she didn't feel pain or anxiety or fear but felt only the goodness that comes from an altered consciousness, but instead, she took a deep breath, and she kept on walking through the cold dark night, and she knew Kylie was probably already at home by now, with her husband her pets and yet Angie… Angie just kept striding into the darkness, wondering when her turn would come. (319)

A Perfect Sunday Afternoon
A true story in one sentence
by Diane H. Larson

THE FAMILY WAS ENJOYING A PEACEFUL Sunday afternoon, with Mom in the kitchen putting last minute touches on dinner, the roast in the oven sending delicious smells wafting toward her brood who were gathered in front of the woodstove in the open family area nearby, the cozy fire radiating light and warmth over Duffy, their small dog, sleeping in her bed in front of the fire, eight-year-old Julianne, curled up in one corner of the L-shaped couch, her stuffed tiger snuggled against her, quietly reading, no doubt one of her favorite Judy Blume books, Dad, sleepily reading the Sunday paper in another corner of the couch, his long legs stretched out next to Duffy, and ten-year-old Kenny, sitting cross-legged on the rug in front of the couch, intensely focused on a special project that had kept him busy for the past couple of hours, as he ever so carefully sorted hundreds of his precious baseball cards into their particular years and teams, creating tidy piles of cards neatly stacked across the rug in front of him, all in readiness for the arrival of Mom's parents, who were joining them to share a happy Sunday dinner together, a bucolic scene indeed, when the sound of the doorbell broke the silence, simultaneously causing Julianne to jump up and hurry out of the room to open the front door, Dad to fold up the newspaper and set it aside, Duffy to wake up and bark in great excitement as she dashed across Kenny's meticulous piles, scattering his cards hither and yon around the rug, and Kenny, to sit for one moment in stunned silence staring blankly at the mess Duffy had created, inadvertently allowing time for his very staid and proper British grandfather to step into the doorway of the room and view the scene, before letting loose with the worst string of profanity any ten-year-old boy could muster, words Mom didn't even know he knew, and when she looked toward the doorway, she saw her father's somber face turn pale, and she sighed to herself, thinking that the timing could not have been more perfect. (353)

Cinnamon Bear
by Suezy Proctor

MY FAVORITE HIKING MEMORY is a magic moment in the late summer of 1983 when I was hiking Loup Loup Pass (elev. 4020 ft.) located in the state of Washington, east of the Methow Valley of Okanogan County, between the towns of Twisp and Okanogan on State Route 20, where a small ski area is located at the top of the pass and where, on this particular day, it was 78-degrees with a gentle breeze that carried traces of sun-ripened berries, sweet grass, and wood smoke from someone's fireplace miles away, when after four hours of solid climbing and switchbacks, I took a rest on a rather large, wide, smooth rock, the perfect roost for lunch with an incredible down-valley view, the perfect time and place to grab my journal out of my pack to record the passionate conversations I'd had with myself that day, occasionally looking up and out into the distance to clear my mind, and it was one of those moments that the magic happened when I saw movement, but didn't really recognize what it was that I was seeing as I strained for clarity, and when it came into focus it revealed, blended in with the grasses, the reddish-brown coat of a majestic cinnamon bear, lumbering and lollygagging as it swiped at the bees on the flowering thistle, then rolling down a small hill like a rolled-up carpet, again and again and again, as I sat transfixed, trying not to move because, let's face it, the bear outweighed me by a few hundred pounds and I was content right where I sat, but as time went on, it eventually moved on, and as you can imagine I was relieved when it did, because I had little time to make it over the top and down the other side to catch my ride back into town, knowing that when I did get home, I would come back to this memory often and visualize sitting on that wide, smooth rock as I breathed in the sweetest smells, looking up and out toward the valley below, waiting… waiting… waiting… to see the cinnamon bear once again. (359)

When Will We Stop Pretending?
by Jennifer Schneider

I SET MY ALARM FOR 6:30 A.M. but it might as well be broken because my kids awoke at six and the dog, he was up since 5:30 (must have forgotten I had let the poor thing out at three), so by seven we were packed and ready for the bus, and surprisingly I made it to work on time despite the exhausting traffic that came as a welcome turn of events right up until the moment I remembered tonight was "date night" (I don't know the origins of the term, but I'm convinced "date night" was coined by marketers for the profit-seeking restaurant business, especially those owned by bachelors) and I thought *when will others stop pretending... when can I?* since after work there was homework, soccer, and dinner for which I was no longer hungry because finishing the kids' leftovers took care of that, and next I had the joys of having to squeeze into one of the many too-snug dresses that hung in the far recesses of my closet (most of which was full of lonely fabrics, dresses, and skirts for which I no longer had any real use and which fit neither me nor current fashion trends), and that's when my husband walked in the door looking drained and happy to be home, and still five minutes later we were on our way (after all, it was "date night") to meet friends at a new place that had come with raving reviews, which I should have realized that my friends' *pretending* knows no bounds because we paid $24 for a plate of roast chicken and potatoes that bore an uncanny resemblance to the overcooked, slightly burnt meal I had prepared a few hours earlier, causing me to feel irritable and offended, although not as mad as my husband, who was struggling to hide his rising annoyance at the expense, but I knew because our exhausted faces easily revealed our dismay, and finally we both breathed a long and silent relief when we paid the bill and headed home, wanting nothing more than our kids, our old sweats, and sleep, when I asked myself again, *why do we all pretend?* (363)

Watermelon
by Jessica Schulz

AT THE NEIGHBORHOOD FRUIT AND VEGETABLE stand, enthralled with the variety, I found myself face to face with two bins of gargantuan watermelons, one seedless and the other seeded and priced, according to the handwritten signs, $6 for seedless and $7 (a dollar more) for seeded, and was reminded, I could actually taste the sweetness of watermelons of days gone by, all that despite the annoying presence of seeds always seemed to embody the taste of summer, so I unhesitatingly hoisted, not without considerable effort, one of those green, seed-filled, submarine-sized orbs, and headed to the checkout stand where the lady kindly offered to hand carry it into my car so I could exit on the road leaving the fruit stand but, like a fool, I insisted on carrying it to my car, along with all of my other purchases (strawberries, new potatoes, ripe tomatoes) and as you could probably predict, I dropped the darned thing as I was almost to my car and it made a horrible noise — SPLAT — as it thudded to the ground and split open, all of its advertised seeds and juicy fruit visible, whereupon I carefully picked up the cracked melon, juice running down my arm, and carried it back to the fruit stand to ask for a bag but the lady felt duty-bound to give me a new one and insisted, as she carefully placed the injured melon (which she planned to have for dinner), in a box before going to find me a replacement, and that this time she would hand my new seeded melon carefully to me in my car, ensuring that it would make it safely home (or at least off the premises), which it did, and I carried it safely to my kitchen counter, where after cutting into the monstrous thing (no easy trick because it was bigger than my cutting board) I discovered it to be dry in the middle with large sections of baggy, saggy pink flesh, but luckily had some usable portions attached to the outer rim, and despite the fact that there were lots of seeds, the melon was unimpressive and bland-tasting, nothing like the seeded melons of my youth, and I regretted having paid the extra dollar...(374)

Swallowing
by Babz Clough

SHE TRIED TO SWALLOW, but her throat seemed to close shut and the inability to swallow induced panic and made her try even harder to breathe and swallow and talk, but her throat was stuck and she moved her head from side to side as if that might unstick the dry, stuck insides, but it made no difference and then the big white blob of a woman appeared at her bedside, murmuring something and Maria stopped moving her head long enough to try and decipher what the woman was saying and to try to mutter "water" but it all came out as a senseless whisper and the big white blob shook her head slowly saying, "No water, not yet, but here, try an ice chip," and Maria felt the cool liquid slide along her lips and onto her parched tongue and felt the water melt and slip as her throat widened just a bit, but she still couldn't quite swallow, and she whispered out "more" and the white-robed woman slid another chip onto Maria's tongue, whispering "Easy, easy, you're okay," and this time Maria felt the cool water trickling into the dark, dry space under her tongue and one cool drop against her teeth, and this time the water didn't so much trickle down her throat because she actively swallowed it, feeling the little muscles ripple in her throat, and when it was gone, she could finally moan out something that resembled "thank you", and with this the woman put a straw into the pink plastic pitcher on the rolling tray and lifted up Maria, just an inch or so off the rough white sheets that smelled of bleach and disinfectant and said, "Try taking one small sip" and Maria could do that, a sip of her own volition, using her dry and cracked lips to suck the water up through the straw and actually drink, all under her own strength and coordination, and the nurse slowly let her rest back against the pillows of the hospital bed before saying to her, "You overdosed, Maria" and she knew at that point that although she'd OD'd, someone had been around with Narcan or something to bring her back to this world of familiarity and disappointment. (374)

Deferred Judgment
by Jennifer Schneider

A FEW WEEKS BACK, while I watched a live blacksmith's demonstration, I heard a young girl exclaim, "Whoa, that's cool, what makes the wood turn…", and she asked again while another added, "won't it fall off…" **while** the blacksmith worked with purpose, focusing on his craft, apparently oblivious to (or determined to ignore) their inquiries, but the girls, with a curiosity so strong and so pure that nothing could deter them, continued to question "why is there a pipe… what does it do… when will the smoke stop…" **until** finally the blacksmith offered a weak attempt at a smile, with not a hint of encouragement and declared, "that's it folks" dismissing us, lesson over, no more questions, no answers, which irritated me and offended both the young girls on whose behalf I wondered, what if two boys inquired instead, and that's why a week later, I returned, this time, noticing the group was larger, with a cluster of boys gathered near the front, their faces just as curious as the young girls who preceded them, displaying an eagerness manifested in torsos and limbs draped across the bannister, and soon the questions began, like last time, the kids in the front with the best view, the most eager and the most inquisitive asking, "why does it take so long…, how come you wear gloves…, who built the pipe…", the boys begged to know, and I waited and listened for a response from the blacksmith, but his reaction was no different than with the young girls, and I realized that I wasn't sure what I had expected, asking myself if I have become so cynical, so consumed by the research and the affronts I know to be real that I fail to remember that some injustices are gender blind, while understanding that the blacksmith should have responded to all of the questions, which left me wondering if I judge too quickly (do I look for discrimination where there is none to be had) and began to offer excuses, such as: maybe he wasn't feeling well, maybe he was deep in concentration, maybe it was something else, and I wasn't sure, but next time I'll wait longer before judging, not because discrimination isn't real, but because not all issues are gender specific, not all slights are intentional, and not all questions need answers. (390)

This Is Who I Am
by Nick Page

THE LIFE OF A SEMI-COLON can be lonely indeed, something useless and unwanted, unloved and unneeded, a sense of guilt plaguing its existence, a sense of purposelessness, longing to make sense, jealous of the comma, jealous of the exclamation point, envious of the always-elusive question mark, and yet aware it is what it is, overused, yes, but used just the same and sometimes proudly by maverick dreamers and academic spoilers alike, and yet always longing for its fate, knowing the end will come as it does for us all, those with usefulness and those redundant of use, those building great crescendos of wisdom and those caught in the repetitive dullness of clichés, and when the end comes, there is but the briefest of spaces, two to be exact, before the next reiteration of thought extracts itself from the mind of its creator, the wordsmith, the crafty player of dreams, the writer who knows that he too will meet his end and that his end, perhaps suddenly, will honor and salute the almighty period, but here's the rub, for our friend the semi-colon is wanting change, is desperately seeking an honesty of being, an authenticity of self, for she no longer identifies as being a semi-colon, an identity forced upon her against her will, and it is her life's purpose to become the greatest of all punctuations, that purveyor of finality known as our almighty period, that little dot that is so small and yet so complete in its finite infinity, the last word, the end of all dreams, and our semi-colon, fearful of the world's reaction to her coming out as a period, fearful of what her parents, the colons, will say, her cousins, the quotation marks, very opinionated, her cruel aunts and uncles, the dashes and the slashes, and she even doubts herself, but she knows that being a trans-punctuation or even bi-punctual, will shape her core for she knows that being a semi-anything simply is not who she is and so she takes her stand and she shouts out, "I am not a semi-colon and I am not a passing symbol of transition from one phrase to another because I am the end, the symbol of wholeness concluded, of self-aware finality, and I have said what I must say and that is that and this is who I am; period." (392)

I'm Still Here at 85
(Apologies to Stephen Sondheim and the Broadway musical "Follies")
by Stanley Krippner, PhD

GOOD TIMES AND BAD TIMES:
I've seen them all and, my dear,
I'm still here!
Born in depressed times,
Our parents' love was sincere,
So I'm here…

I did some hard work
On our farm,
Apples were a perk,
As for harm,
School bullies left me in fear,
It was drear…

Had fifteen presidents,
Seen most of them but not Trump
(Please don't jeer)…
My fourteen residences
Gave me a place to lie down,
So I'm here…

My universities
Were the best,
All the diversity
Taught me the rest;
Never had time to get depressed,
Nowhere near,

Tons of schoolwork kept me in gear
I'm no seer and

I've worked with children
Having some trouble to learn,
Then went to Brooklyn,
Giving dream research a turn,
But left for Saybrook where
Each year I return
'Cause it's near, and

I've seen Bing Crosby,
Sinatra, and Elvis too,
Also Bill Cosby,
Elton, the "Stones" and the "Who"
And Tallulah Bankhead who
Called me "dahling"
Then went to the loo as
I stayed put
With a leer…

I've heard John Lennon and Paul McCartney,
Yes, that was fun-and-a half,
But when you've heard Joseph and Eugene McCarthy
Anything else is a laugh…
I've been to Spain and
One hundred countries and more,
Far and near, and
I've been in pain,
Two car wrecks with blood and gore,
But I'm here…

Worked with veterans
From six wars,
Interviewed shamans,
Psychics, and whores,

Also astronauts,
(None of them bores),
Saw the Iron Curtain disappear,
Shed no tear, of course…

Met Robin Williams
Right on the streets of New York,
And Ethel Merman
While her fans started to gawk,
Knew Alan Watts,
Met Lucille Ball,
Own a chunk of the Berlin Wall,
On China's Great Wall, I took a walk,
Lend an ear…

Twice I've seen Marilyn Monroe,
Sure, that was fun-and-a-half,
Plus Madonna and Marilyn Manson
Always good for a laugh,
I've met Martin King, Junior
Tried to follow his road,
I've seen two Popes and the Dalai Lama
But don't share their abode,
Hung out with rock stars,
The Grateful Dead and their crew,

And Frank Lloyd Wright
(he was from Wisconsin too)
Spent time with grandkids,
Gratefully I have two,
As I turned eight-five
But look ninety-two,
Yet I'm here…

I've run the gamut,
ESP to LSD,
Three cheers and damn it,
As the French say, "C'est la vie"
I got through all of last year
Quite severe,
God knows at least I was there,
And time goes on…
And I'm still here! (419)

Are You Hungary?
by Geoffrey Williams

SITTING IN THE FLAT AS J PREPARED the thick sliced lobster sandwiches from thick sliced lobsters and brown bread because I don't like rolls, I declared it was time to set out for Jakarta, and did so forthwith, if not sooner, steering the ship carefully through the steep and windy, not to mention (so I won't) crowded streets of the town until at a particularly dicey crossroads my way was blocked by a removal lorry which was neither removing nor delivering, but to all intents and purposes not moving, thereby forcing me to steer my ship up a one-way street the wrong way as there was really no means of doing otherwise as large ships simply don't do reverse, and anyway I didn't think any oncoming traffic was going to challenge me as I sailed majestically between the badly parked cars and down towards the beach where I duly parked the ship on the sand whilst waiting for J to turn up with the freshly made sandwiches without which it would have been impossible to have travelled all the way to Jakarta, wherever that might be, as I had clean forgotten to take any maps or charts, because these seafaring people of which I am not, call these useful pieces of paper into which it would be a shame to wrap fish and chips as the vinegar does make the print run so, although I must admit some form of sustenance would have been nice whilst sitting on the hot sand and chatting with the dry cleaner's man who brought all of J's clothes neatly hanging on hangers on one of those nicely covered trolley things they have in hotels, but not so much on ships as they roll all over the place in heavy seas, not that I foresee a rough passage as we'll use only canals as I did, proudly standing at the helm from where I steered the vessel through narrow channels, moaning about the heat because she was wearing freshly laundered appropriate clothing while I was still clad in thick, well-creased flannel trousers until, upon J's suggestion I disrobed and, comfortably nude and cool, retook my place at the helm and, since even I knew that customs men were unaccustomed to bareness and that lock keepers lacked levity, I could, should the need arise, always wrap myself in that chart which was still ungreased from the fish and chips that I had never eaten and which meant I was a mite hungry, which is odd as I don't think Jakarta is in Hungary, or is it? (431)

January
by Judy Ashley

JANUARY IS A PLEASANT MONTH and I think it's probably my favorite and not just because my birthday is in January (when my friends take me to lunch and sometimes I get presents as well as lots of funny cards) or because my hubby also has a birthday this month, but because it is a quiet month when the holidays are past and my house is once again restored to its natural comfortableness decluttered of silly Santas and adorable stockings with names lovingly hand-stitched on each one, and lighted garlands, and a very large tree in the middle of my living room and other sundry holiday decorations strewn about the rooms and there are no more holiday gatherings that often can become stressful and sometimes even meaningless in the loudness and hurriedness of it all, what with adding multiple tasks and projects to our already normally busy schedules and leaving us with no free time at all, and then trying to coordinate everyone's conflicting schedules so that the whole family can be together at least one day during this time and the worry over appropriate gifts, as well as the extra money spent that probably should not have been spent and, of course, I cannot forget all those tasty holiday treats that take us away from our normal eating habits and often make us feel not so great but yet, I must admit that I did, and I do, enjoy the holidays and all of the festivities that surround them from October through December, and I know that I will enjoy them again when they roll around next year even though I will be thinking that we just did this and how can it be time to do it all again, but I will joyously do it again and I will appreciate and take pleasure in the delights of my grandchildren, grandnieces, grandnephews and any other wide-eyed child (from 1 to 99) delighting in the magic of the holiday season, and I too will be thrilled with the magic and will happily watch magical Christmas movies late into the night when my preparations have been completed, and I shall make cookies and attend special holiday events and before I know it, once again it will be January, which is a month I love because it is calm and cold, which makes hanging out at home such a pleasure when I can regroup and refocus and perhaps even read a book or write a one-sentence story and, well, simply enjoy being in the moment and, of course, if it were not for those hectic holiday weeks, I would not be able to enjoy January as much as I do, now would I? (451)

Martin
by Debbie Davidson

MARTIN HAD A KNACK FOR NUMBERS, always adding and subtracting or multiplying and dividing something, most times just to keep his self-confidence up since his daddy rarely said anything except, "Boy, give me yo' money," from the part-time job he had after school when he was young, which Martin begrudgingly gave to him because Pops was small, but he was mighty powerful with a muscular build yielding arms only someone as large as Mohammed Ali should have had and hands the size of The Hulk to go along with a mouth so vulgar even longshoremen cringed at the profanity emitting from that little man's mouth, and Pops was aware of the impact he had on people but he didn't care because life hadn't done much for him in Tennessee and he never could afford to leave or even have enough courage to try, so he just complained daily for sixty-five years that he didn't get that longshoreman's job because he was black, as if he chose his skin color, but Martin and his two brothers were all over six feet tall, almost as if God made them that way so they had a chance living with a father as ornery as Pop who beat his wife, their mother, for the last time when the three brothers, led and egged on by Martin to join him in defying Pop by kicking his butt if Pop "ever put his hands on Mom again," so the beatings stopped and Mom stayed with Pop, but Martin didn't figure that his brothers would stay under Pop's rule, but they did, however neither amounted to much — like Pop, just sitting around complaining about unfairness in life and the heat in Tennessee — but Martin with his ability to calculate, calculated his destiny away from Pops by joining the Army and then finally residing in Washington state more miles than he dared calculate away from Pop's influence, but he never calculated illness in his equation or Linda, his wife, who was ten years younger, dying from cancer, when he confidently said in Pop's face forty-five years ago when he left for the Army, "I ain't never moving back home," and now he may have to eat his words since kidney failure, diabetes, and heart disease have all begun to take their toll on his ability to care for himself, even his ability to wipe his own butt as he lay, yet again, in another hospital bed (too many times to calculate) since his health began accelerating downwards a year after Linda's death, and now his eyes bloodshot from hidden tears, Martin lay wondering how his calculations could have been so far off, and his memory irreconcilably weakened by multiple illnesses could only focus long enough to remind him again and again that he had a problem he needed to solve. (472)

A Cautionary Tale
A true story in one sentence
by Diane H. Larson

ONE BRIGHT AND SUNNY DAY in August, Himself, tired after years of hacking away at the blackberry jungle growing down below our house, and ever hopeful that he wouldn't pick up his annual horrendous case of poison oak, suddenly decided that there had to be a better option, so he came up with what he thought was a brilliant idea, that burning down the blackberry bushes would speed up the job and save him a lot of time and trouble, and once this bee got in his cap, no cautionary words, like maybe this wasn't his wisest idea, could get through to him, though he did think to pull a hose to what he must have supposed was within spraying distance of the blackberries before he doused them with kerosene, cast a match... and his caution... to the wind, and waited to see what would happen, and meanwhile, I stood watching from the back deck of our house up above, my heart in my throat as the wind caught the flames and the bushes began to burn, slowly at first, and then, within an amazingly short time, bursting into an enormous wall of fire, resulting in my seeing visions of all the tall fir trees around us... our house... and the whole neighborhood going up in flames, while at the same time, Himself must have realized that perhaps this was something he had not thought all the way through, so he grabbed the hose, only to discover that its spray halted short of the bushes, and when he ran to get our longer hose, he suddenly remembered something he had unfortunately forgotten, that our neighbors' well had broken down, and they had borrowed our long hose and our water to use until their well could be repaired, so he had to try to find a second shorter hose to attach to the first one, which took some time, and meanwhile the bushes continued to burn higher and hotter, such that I was pacing back and forth on the deck like a crazed wild animal, wondering whether I should call the fire department, and when he got back, I yelled this question at him, but he yelled back, "No, not yet!" as he got the hoses connected and started spraying water at the blazing blackberry bushes, while I continued to frantically yell at him that we needed to call the fire department and to wonder if I should make the call without his agreement, so it was unbelievably fortunate that putting the two hoses together, plus the fact that we have extremely powerful water pressure, worked, as the flames finally began to recede in response to the steady stream of water, and after a time, it was apparent that he had the fire under control, whereupon I breathed an enormous sigh of relief, my heart still pounding like a jackhammer, though I was pretty sure that my heart was not pounding nearly as fast as his! (495)

Hey!
by Anne Wood

It started in my cheeks, this warmth, as it flushed them red just from making eye contact with him from across the bar, through the smoke and noise being created and breathed by people we probably both know (because Huntsville is small enough for that to be an unsurprising reality), and from my cheeks it spread to my ears that were all the sudden hot as if I was embarrassed, but I know I wasn't because none of this felt uncomfortable or bad as the warmth traveled from my head to my stomach (which actually did feel like it had butterflies around inside) and then to my appendages — arms to shaky hands, legs to unsteady feet — but noticeably skipping over my chest as if my head was its own rebel entity protesting the whole thing, not by screaming or yelling or even being cold, but rather just by a total lack of participation in this consuming, silly warmth as if it has decided to take a knee in a confounding display of simultaneous defiance and nonchalance, somehow communicating both indifference and a refusal to be wooed by his Robert Redford smile with those charmingly crooked teeth that are framed by full lips and rosy cheeks and crows-feet eyes that are staring right at me, inviting me to smile back at him through the smoke that was doing absolutely nothing to dull his shine or cloud our connection, which probably was grossly apparent to everyone in that bar who saw us staring at each other, smiling like a couple of idiots, until — oh god — he starts to move across the bar floating through the smoke, weaving through the crowd of bodies (all of which turn pale next to him), getting closer and closer to the back corner where I sat with my flushed cheeks and burning ears and shaky hands that have just knocked over my beer onto the already disgusting table that is unofficially reserved for awkward wallflowers like me who apparently spill on it often enough that the barkeep doesn't bother to clean it, so the only reason I am trying to (vainly, mind you) is that I can literally feel him getting closer and can think of nothing less romantic than two people sopping up cheap beer, or worse… one person doing it, me, if he decides not to approach the mess after all because maybe he doesn't like messes, and yes I'm referring to both the literal mess that is my table and the figurative mess that is my life, but apparently he is unafraid of messes because the next time I look up from the most recent mess I have created, he's right in front of me, and I can feel that warmth that started in my cheeks instantly explode into my chest, into my bored, guarded, indifferent heart, with a start and a spark and a gasp like it has been awakened from the deepest sleep at the moment he looked at me and said, "Hey." (502)

The Night the Doodlebug Hit
by Angela Richardson

It was 1943, so I was told, and the second world war was raging, when on this particular evening with no sirens sounding and only the enormous search lights that lit up the skies to show enemy planes approaching London were visible, moving north and south and from east to west, constantly on the lookout, and it was apparently the silence and the eerie quiet that was making my father nervous, restless, and ill-at-ease, and which caused him to tell my mother, "Let's go, and immediately so we can have time to go down the road to the Casselman's nearby house," and "I'll get Angela," and that was when I was awakened by a strong arm lifting me from my baby bed, and I heard urgent whispers, and shushing sounds and words like "Hurry, hurry, don't forget her Panda bear or she'll have a fit when she wakes up," which nobody needed to have worried about because I was already wide awake as I was hoisted from my bed, along with Panda, and both of us tucked safely underneath my father's arm, which was not too comfortable, but I made no protest as the atmosphere around us, the whispering, an occasional flashlight shining briefly that caused someone to say, "Put that out, put that out, no light because we'll be seen," seemed to fill my very young senses, and being uncomfortable for the moment was the least of my problems as we went out into the chilly night air, with my father almost running, taking big long strides to get to the Casselman house as fast as he could, with my mother running along behind him, saying things like "Have you got her?" and "Don't drop her," and words that loving mothers would say, until we finally arrived safely, where I remember voices saying, "She'll go back to sleep," and "Isn't she an angel?", as I was wrapped in warm blankets and I remember nothing more of that night, though my parents' memories were vivid indeed, for fifteen minutes after our arrival. . . or so they tell me. . . I had been put to bed, and the kettle had been put on, and the tea spooned into a heated teapot, when a V2 German bomber, known as a "doodlebug" hit our house head-on, a perfect hit, causing the house to disappear, as well as parts of my father's car, which were subsequently found half a mile away, leaving the foundation as the only thing remaining besides — by the grace of God — the family that dwelt therein, so that when my composer father wrote the "London Fantasia" a couple of years later, he put a siren in his concerto and told an interviewer on a radio show he was asked to do some years later for the BBC, that he heard a voice clearly tell him that fateful night, "Get out, and get out now!" a voice he obeyed instantly, and thank Heavens he did, or I should not be here to tell you this tale. (508)

Carbon Forest
(Jamai's Travelogue)
by Michael Robbins

THE TREE SEEMED ENGORGED on the wastes of our society, indeed she was visible in her respiration, the deep emerald trunk expanding and contracting while I stood at the front of roots burrowing in a hundred-meter radius around it, oddly leading to the whimsy that I could destroy her with a single thought, but that's not what I was about, so I deposited the penlight, even my shoes (anything remotely threatening, really) into my shoulder bag that was abandoned on the trail 200 meters behind and, as I padded shoeless to the tree, I reflected that the people of this island were long gone, swept away centuries ago by the ocean, although their echoes remained, every terror of their last moments a physical stain that had virtually wrapped a fist around my spirit and drew me to this island slowly rising from the sea, centuries after so much life had been wiped out by our maleficence, but conversely life evolved as it would, adapting to the carbon choking our atmosphere, the air forcing our children to walk in rebreather masks, all the while giving birth to flora such as this that was able to take advantage of our atmospheric excesses to achieve new spasms of growth, yet with gifted eyes I viewed all the dead drawn to the tree, seeking comfort in her branches, visible to me as colorless after-images of lives long vanished, an attraction not lost to me since her presence was so prominent it was easy to forget she was still a plant (albeit an extraordinarily large one) stretching a hundred meters to the sky, plus she had no intelligence as we understood it, but almost certainly an awareness of the localized environment and of her presence, small as that was, for while I clambered over those supple bare roots I wondered whether she sensed a kindred spirit, after all, it was for this reason I traveled, alone, on a journey not of adventure but discovery, now that I was widowed and our children grown, there was nothing to keep me home, and now reality intruded with the waxy vine twining around my wrist, another settling around the waist, joined to an awareness of buds tasting perspiration, drawing her own conclusions from my biochemical secretions, but of this she need not fear even as the vine knotted snugly to my middle and drew me into her roots, which to be honest wouldn't have been the first time for this sort of thing, except in this case I was under obligation, one I accepted willingly, nodding to the new god, though plainly she couldn't possibly observe this for the truth was that this was the sixth such site I'd visited, and as with elsewhere, this tree was now under my protection, and I trust the first Ax-Man exploding would be sufficient warning to all others, but for tonight I was tired, nestling to my new acquaintance's trunk as her roots enfolded my knees while a limb brushed past my shoulder to dump the shoulder bag within easy reach near my right ankle and vents in her trunk opened, blowing mists of fresh oxygen around me. (527)

Delay
by Nick Romeo

I SIT HERE TRYING TO SIGNAL PEOPLE for help by making as many sounds and movements as possible, since it is difficult to move with this much rope tied around me, and it is hard to talk, let alone scream with this ball-gag wedged in my mouth, when truly, all I wanted was some assistance from the customer service reps, but I guess they got offended when I refused their offers of stale snacks and tap water straight from the bathroom urinal — excuse me if I'm still full from McDonald's — and now I watch people enter the building, pretending that they don't notice me, while I'm obviously in a predicament, as they casually step in line to be helped, not making eye contact with me, and yes, the people walk in off the street, sometimes even stepping on my feet as they pass, and then step in line to get helped, and the people at the windows gleefully introduce themselves to these people off the street before they go through a spiel about offers for the month and how these random people off the street can save a boat-load of money, in fact, money will rain on them for forty days and forty nights drowning them, their family, and their pets with money, and they will need to build a boat to save themselves from the boatload of money that will rain down from the sky, and I listen politely, not that I have a choice, and wait for someone to help me, but all I hear is Michael Bolton being played over the loud speaker (it must be Michael Bolton Day because they have played the same song about nine-hundred times), but wait, I think I see the manager now as she is being carried on a throne made of gold with emerald and ruby accents by several men with ripped muscles and wearing Tarzan-styled swim trunks, while the man in the lead drops roses on the ground and the man trailing picks up the roses, stashing them neatly in a plastic bag, and watch now as she tells them to halt, then jumps off her throne and prances toward me and, within an inch from my face she screams, "What do you have to say for yourself?" as the buff muscly men encircle me, so I respond, "I'm sorry for bouncing my check, and I was wondering if you could waive the late fee, overdraft fee, and release my mom from your prison, which doubles as your safe deposit vault?" at which she leans back and releases a deep guttural laugh that causes the walls to shake and the safety glass in the front window to crack, and then the super-muscle-bound minions follow her lead and laugh in unison before she snaps her fingers and they hush, and all the people off the street freeze, along with the customer service reps who were in midsentence with the latest pitch, and they stare too as she replies, "I have a better idea," and reaches inside her purple robe to reveal a mini gas-powered chainsaw, and fires it up to full power as she shouts to her men, "Now grab his arm"... (533)

Delicate Balance
by Debbie Davidson

I FELT THE URGE TO GET UP OFF MY BIG BUTT to do the much dreaded "yard work" while there was still daylight because looking at that bosky area dominated by my overgrown unkempt laurel hedge one more day as I peered out the sliding glass door would drive me battier than sitting in front of the boob tube to be influenced by targeted advertisements and programs designed to exploit our minds to spend that last dollar we saved for our children or a night out with that special person, but these programs seize your subconscious so that you feel compelled to go online or to a store to exonerate your mind of the spending compulsion, knowing it is a temporary fix to curb your appetite for that stupid product you didn't need but just this one time while you work it out you will buy the object of your desire just to feel momentarily better, however, rather than allowing myself to be further tempted to s-p-e-n-d, I decided to do the deplorable enervating outside chore, trim that despicable hedge that appears to have grown larger since deciding to step outside, rather than torture my mind meditating on why I shouldn't just buy one more thing, so instead of giving into the advertisement induced compulsion, I envision my hedge looking spectacular while I grudgingly claim my tools from the garage as I get into the "yard beautification mood", turn on the hedge trimmer, and begin shaping that monstrosity that then starts to take on its natural beauty and shape, so much so that my chest begins to poke out with pride, however, my thoughts begin to center in on this irritating chirping emanating from the direction of my apple tree that at first addles my brain then begins to annoy me because I need to concentrate to ensure I don't cut the power cord and blow a fuse again, but the source of my annoyance continues making cavil, unrelenting chirps causing me to ignore my sub-conscience then conscience admonitions because I felt more powerful than all the fervor in that tiny finch trying to get my attention, so consequently I became more intent on trimming that hedge knowing she was trying to tell me something that I didn't want to hear as she bravely hopped from one branch to another then onto the ground near me, as close as she dared, sounding out one last chirp before flying back to the apple tree as I began blowing away the last of the leaves I'd cut from that laurel hedge when I spotted something pale blue, small, slightly oblong beneath a few of the remaining cut leaves that had fallen on the ground, and I realized why that finch was talking to me, warning me that I was going to expose her babies to predators, and tears ran down my face as I grasped what my stubborn pride had done and I was overwhelmed with grief, and the beauty in my trimmed laurel hedge now meant nothing as I comprehended how delicate a balance humans and the rest of nature share and how haphazardly people take for granted our right to do what we please without consideration of that delicate balance. (540)

Enough for Merle and Me
by Joanne Johnston Francis

ALL THAT'S LEFT STILL TO BUY for Thanksgiving dinner is here on my list in my coat pocket or maybe here in my pocketbook or lord have mercy did I leave it on the kitchen counter there beside our little grandbaby Gordy's goldfishes, but no problem for I can quickly call Merle and get him to read off my list to me if he's not already out in the barn spoiling that old swayback horse of his, but is this not the beauty of the age we live in — a cell phone in every pocketbook and every pocket, the perfect hedge for the list we write and too often forget to take to the market, the list we took such care with, organizing it into paper products and what-not from the pharmacy, housekeeping goods, and package goods (what we here in the south call certain high-octane beverages and brown-bag to the restaurant and always vote up in our local option election not to have to drive all the way down the mountain to the bootleg man, if you must know), and just in case you find it amusing, I'm not able to locate my cell phone in my pocketbook where I know I left it, and let me just tell you straight away I don't much cotton to carrying a cell phone with me every place for obvious reasons, among them the looks to kill you get at the movie theater when it goes to ringing and worse yet how we get to depending on it when all we really need is concentration on what we know we wrote only yesterday or was it the day before starting with caviar and cream cheese and radishes, see what I mean — not all that hard once we concentrate — plus horse radish for the cranberry relish and then some kind of hot pepper jelly just in case there's somebody don't care to eat fish roe, but did I not already get the pepper jelly yesterday and maybe we can live without the fish roe and make do with some other recipe so I can get the heck out of here before these check-out lines gets any longer and I'm not fit company and can't think of one single thing on this earth to be thankful for so why even go over to Merle's sister's new boyfriend's mama's big two-story brick home by the river she got from the settlement but only by being some kind of kin to the insurance man, and just fix us two a tuna plate with pickles and tater chips, two scoops of vanilla and a chocolate cookie for our own private Thanksgiving, build us a little coal fire in the parlor stove, shut off the electric and light some candles, put some music on the CD player, and two-step into tomorrow and come morning get up with the sun like we do every day and fix us a good stout pot of coffee and bake us some good bread pudding and fry us up some of Merle's sausage and some apples off of our last two Virginia Beauty apple trees there by the woodshed the county liked to took out when they put the new road through, a big old country breakfast and just enough for him and me. (552)

We Were on the Same Page
by Donna Lee Anderson

THAT'S WHAT I SORTA THOUGHT TOO, I mean exactly what she said, that Jim was probably just late coming home from work and when he did get home he'd be able to clear up this misunderstanding that was happening between his girlfriend and me, not that it needed clearing up, because I'm not sure she knew that I was Jim's wife and that this week Jim was supposed to be on a fishing trip in Canada, but she said he told her he'd be home around six o'clock and it was now six-thirty, so I asked her again where he was and she said she thought he was on his way home from work now, at least he was at work when she called him earlier around four o'clock to ask him to bring home a bottle of rum so they could celebrate his news of being single again, but he said he'd rather go out to dinner in Seattle so she should be ready and they'd go to the Space Needle and really do it up right, but she told him she was afraid of heights, so then he said for her to pick out a place for them to go, and when I got here I could see through the window she was looking on-line, but when I rang the bell she put down the laptop and came to answer it and now here I was and she didn't know what to tell me because she was all dressed in this blue sheath that was really tight in the right places, and was all ready for Jim to get home so they could leave and maybe catch the seven o'clock ferry, but Jim wasn't coming home and I knew that because I left Jim in the parking lot at the wharf where he worked, except he had a shot-gun bullet in his head, so I knew he wasn't just late, he wouldn't be coming home to her at all, and the trip to Seattle wouldn't happen tonight because I'd brought the shot-gun here too, and although I'd left it on the porch, it was very handy, and within easy reach, but because she hadn't invited me in or even asked me who I was when she started to shut the door, all the while apologizing to me and saying "I'll be right back," I totally didn't expect her to return, but when she did come back and opened the door she said, "Sorry, Nature called and how rude of me, making you just stand on the porch while we talked, so come in and wait for Jim and who did you say you were?" but as I stepped inside I could see she had a small pistol in one hand and the phone in the other and then she said, "Yes that's right, she's now in the house and I'm so scared because I saw her bring a shot-gun when she walked up the front path and when I answered the door I could see it leaning against the outdoor porch swing so I played along but now she's inside and I'm so scared," and then she smiled at me but started screaming into the phone, "She's coming after me," and she pointed the gun and pulled the trigger… and I never saw it coming. (558)

There Are Cars; Then There Are CARS
by JoAnn Lakin Jackson

WHEN I RECENTLY SAW THE INFORMATION sign in my town proudly announcing their fourth annual electric car show, I was surprised at my sense of looking forward with anticipation for this day to come so I could see these new cars of the future knowing that this is not always the reaction most women have as I seem to, knowing full well I have had a few unique experiences with a number of exciting cars in my lifetime to reflect back on, such as loving to ride up into the nearby canyons when we lived in Salt Lake City in the 12-cylinder 1937 Lincoln Zephyr my parents had when I was in elementary school to view fields of blue flowers in the spring, frightening but beautiful lightning storms over the city and beyond to the great Salt Lake in the middle of the summer, and my first time viewing skiing at Alta, finishing the day with the car experiencing a vapor lock to be broken by my father sucking on the gas tank leaving a ring of gasoline around his mouth before we safely returned home, which was shortly before I began my first driving lesson in a 1939 Dodge Special at the age of twelve resulting in a drastic effect on our family dog, Friday, who was sitting in the back seat, for when I tried my first back-up it scared him so much he leaped out of the car window, so I had to get out of the car and comfort him to make him relinquish his fear to go on in the future to accompany me and my family on many trips to the mountains and one glorious trip to California many years before the building of Disneyland, which I have never seen, however I'm not sure I've missed it as I have replaced it with memories of driving through the redwood forest, the coastlines of California, Oregon, and Washington in addition to driving in many exciting places such as Los Angeles, San Francisco, Tokyo, and New York City, an event I found to be almost as breathtaking and challenging as the time I drove my fiancé's new 1955 Thunderbird down a yet unopened freeway at 100 miles an hour in the moonlight with the removable top off, that was a truly heart-pounding experience, but I still wish my friend who painstakingly restored a bird's-egg-blue 1937 Delage sporting white leather seats and chrome wheels that had formerly been owned by Peter Ustinov, the actor, would have let me put my two beautiful champion Irish Wolfhounds in the front seat for a photo which would have pleased me as much as another friend taking me out for rides in his Morgan that he was very proud of, and I dare say he is as proud of those two finely crafted hand-made cars as our friend who owns his father's perfectly maintained Model-T both of which are preferable to the intimidatingly low-to-the-ground ride I once had in an Aston Martin during rush hour traffic, but I want you to know I am content and satisfied with my very reliable transportation of today which happens to be a 2006 Toyota Scion — better known as a "toaster" — that we have named "Cranberry", but I suppose I could be fickle minded if I see an especially interesting electric car when I go to the show, we shall see. . . (568)

A Consequence of De-Cluttering
by Joyce Moody

THE IDEA OF DE-CLUTTERING MY HOME was always in the back of my thoughts as something to do when I retired from my full time job because, after all, there just was not enough time in the day to start such an enormous project until I finally had the time and refinanced my house, which needed some repairs inside, and my contractor, Ben, insisted on everything in the living room, dining room, and kitchen being boxed up and stored in the garage where he had built in shelves from the floor to ceiling so he could repair the popcorn ceiling in the living room which he warned would be dusty and messy, followed by replacing the carpet with bamboo flooring which would be another extraordinarily dusty part of the job, but after removing the well-worn and stained carpet, we discovered a beautiful oak hardwood floor looking up at us, so the bamboo flooring was returned to the store and the refurbishing of my home continued with all the furniture moved outside in the front yard, except for my television and one straight-backed chair placed strategically in front of the TV along with a large striped beach towel folded in the middle on the floor for my dog Gany to lie on while I ate sandwiches from the refrigerator and drank water or coffee and longed for one of my smoothies, the kind that are found in the frozen section of any grocery store and all you do is add apple juice and blend, so for days I spent two to three hours in the garage ripping open taped boxes which had not been properly labeled in search of my blender in order to make a smoothie at home, since I had already tried to stir my breakfast drink with my whisk, and shook the juice and protein powder in a cup with a lid (neither of which got the job done) and each morning as I looked in the freezer at my packages for peach, apple, and berry smoothies, I felt progressively irritated that there was no way I could fix one unless I searched the garage again, knowing that somewhere I had a blender and an Osterizer with two speeds, but neither one could be found, so one Saturday morning I decided to go to Target and get the cheapest blender available, however what I saw was a small three-cup chopper and thought, *since I don't have one of those I better purchase it because my blender will certainly turn up and I don't need two of them*, and when I returned home the first thing I did was unbox my chopper, read the directions on the package of frozen berry mix, prepare a cup of apple juice, plug in the chopper, add the ingredients together, turn on the switch and, to my surprise, juice came squirting out of the middle of my new equipment, but that didn't stop me, so I tightened the lid and middle part of the container and watched as the ingredients mixed, turned it off, and poured most of it into a glass, while the rest spilled onto the counter top, sat down, and drank the most wonderful thick berry smoothie I have ever had just to celebrate the work in the house we had accomplished as well as that we identified as the next five projects that will need my attention. (568)

Why Do I Speak Spanish in Public?
by Yazmin Grant

I WAS SITTING WITH MY NEIGHBOR, Selina, and her two friends who happen to be Russian, and as I listened to them speak to each other in Russian, they asked if it bothered me, and I told them no because Spanish was my first language and even though I was left out of their conversation, I understood and it was okay because I knew they were talking in their home language and not trying to be rude because I believe I should never start to give in to other people's fears and insecurities nor force my language expectations on them, which answers that question, "Why Do I speak Spanish in Public?" because no one has the right to force other people to be involved in their conversation, but a considerate person would be thoughtful and respect others in the group because language is a very important part of who you are, and this is especially true if you speak a second language, and for me that language happens to be Spanish, because even though I have lived in this country for more than twenty years, the only way I can preserve my heritage and cultural roots is to speak Spanish every chance I have, even if at the same time I feel that I should not feed into the fear and insecurities of other people because they feel excluded, because when I speak Spanish in your presence, the intent is not be rude or to exclude you from the conversation, it is just me trying to keep that side of me alive because as an Afro-Latina woman, my language is important, like a part of my DNA, my fingerprint, which makes me unique and the longer I live in the USA, the more my language has become a hybrid of Spanish and English as both language and culture blend, which for me is like viewing a coin that has two sides, going back and forth between two cultures, one the place I was born, the other the place I live, as if the seal on one side represents who I am, and the other side shows the way I look that doesn't match the way I sound because I was born in Panama in the mid-sixties and have dark chocolate skin, smooth and shiny like bronze, and hair that is curly, soft, and fluffy like a cotton ball, and I have a short petite build, and most people who don't know me, see me as an Afro-Latina woman… until I open my mouth because I do have a slight accent, but I think my accent is not as heavy as it used to be when I first got here, when I moved from Panama in my early twenties, but I have learned that if I have to speak English just to appease someone else's insecurity that would make me lose a sense of who I am because clearly, stripping away a person's language is like stripping away an important part of their culture because language has a lot to do with our roots and who we are, a part of our DNA that connects with the place where we were born and is rooted in memories of childhood with places, people, food, music, and customs, so I choose to speak Spanish because it helps me stay connected to my childhood in Panama, like going into a time machine, and that's what happens when anyone speaks in public in their native language. (581)

Rosalia
by Sara Jacobelli

So we're sitting at a table at an outdoor café in Palermo, Sicily, me and my gorgeous wife Leola who smells like lilacs as we're celebrating our tenth wedding anniversary and the September air feels like my wife's fingers on my arm and we're drinking Sambuca and who comes up but another one of those young women — one of those panhandling women with a baby… now don't get me wrong, I like babies… okay, me and Leola tried for a few years to have one but nothing happened so we gave up, but this woman was using her baby to try to get money outta dumb American tourists, and me, I see 'em coming a mile away and I always say No, but my wife she's smart and sweet, she's a soft touch and she always gives them a bit of change, you know those little coins that ain't worth much — *spicci* the Sicilians call it — so anyhow this woman she recognizes a pushover when she spots my wife and Leola says, "what a precious baby," and I think she's gonna give this broad a little one- or two- or even five-cent coin and she gives her FIVE WHOLE EUROS and this pisses me off, but that's Leola for you, and the next thing I see is the panhandling woman asks Leola if she wants to hold the kid, and of course Leola says Yes and then I see the lady lean in and whisper in Leola's ear and I'm worried she's gonna talk my smart but sweet wife into giving her more money, and Leola pulls out her purse but there's nothing I can do unless I want a Big Fight with my wife who I love despite it all, and I go to the bathroom (they call it *bagno* here or *toilette)*, so when I come back there's Leola holding the baby, a big-eyed girl in a pink sweater about nine or ten months old and Leola's wiping spittle off the kid's face and smoothing back the kid's dark hair and Leola's got this look in her eyes the same look my kid sister Kimmy used to get when she'd bring home a kitten, and I'm about to say, "No, Leola, you can't keep her," so's I look around and I don't see the baby lady anywhere and I'm trying to think what she looks like — young and skinny, shiny black hair, long purple dress — but there's crowds of people everywhere doing the evening *passeggieta* they call it here, that's when they all go strolling after dinner, and I realize the baby lady is gone, she disappeared, she vanished… poof… and the crowd is swelling, it's some kinda religious festival and there's a parade starting up and a band's playing, with the brass instruments mingling with the musical sound of Sicilian chatter, and I sit down and Leola bounces the baby on her knee and I say, "Are you babysitting?" and she looks at me with those green-blue eyes of hers eyes like a salty sea and she says, "She's ours now, we need to name her, we need to get her a birth certificate so we can put her on my passport, we need to bring her home, Honey, she's ours, and maybe we can name her Rosalia after the Patron Saint of Palermo," and I don't know what to say, but I figure Leola would make a good mamma being so smart and sweet — she's a soft touch — so I order another round of Sambuca — and a glass of milk for the kid. (598)

My Mother the Trekkie
by Suezy Proctor

MY MOTHER WAS A HARD-NOSED BROAD, a female curmudgeon, but all she was really trying to do was compete in a man's world, so she projected this persona, not of a woman in a man's world, but as an equal, nevertheless, and what gave her the notion she could even achieve something like she did came from her fascination of a television show that debuted in the mid-sixties, "Star Trek" and one character in particular, Nyota Uhura, played by Nichelle Nichols, who was an important part of the original series' multicultural crew, because soon after the first scripts for "Star Trek" were being written, Gene Roddenberry, screenwriter and producer of the show, spoke of a new character, a female communications officer, and chose Nichols for the part, and what we all didn't know is that she planned to leave "Star Trek" after its first season, wanting to return to musical theater, instead however, she changed her mind after talking to Martin Luther King, Jr., who was a fan of the show, and who explained that her character signified a future of greater racial harmony and cooperation, saying, "Don't you understand for the first time we're being seen as we should be seen, and you don't have a black role, you have an equal role," and after that precedent, my mother wanted an equal role because, if Uhura could do it, then by golly, so could she, until her mind went to her father who was a CPA by trade, and with him, resistance was futile, but Momma pressed on and worked most of her life in accounting, later earning her CPA license, eventually becoming Okanogan County's Deputy Auditor for three terms, then Chief Accountant until she retired, additionally having her own private CPA practice as well, so it was ironic that when her father died, she was appointed executor of his estate and took over his clients as, meanwhile, I worked for Okanogan County in the Assessor's office during the last few years of her time as Deputy Auditor, which placed us working only a floor apart from one another, and there were the two of us, twenty years apart in age, she at 62, and I at 42 on the day that I walked down the long flight of stairs to the Auditor's office and found her stuck on the third step on her way up, and the closer I got to her, the more aware I became of her physical distress, because she was completely out of breath, her skin was clammy, and all the color was drained from her typically rosy complexion as she held tightly onto the handrail with both hands, and then she did it... she flashed that hard-nosed old broad look at me as if I didn't know the ruse, and I said, "Momma, I'm not going anywhere until I know you're okay," but she kept her deflector shield up, while attempting to tell me she was fine, but shortly after, she uttered an ultimatum, "Do not tell anyone about this, do you understand?" and continued by telling me that she didn't want anyone to see her weakness and for this, she needed to stay strong, that they needed to believe she was who she projected, and as she protested, I thought of Spock and his "live long and prosper", and I mumbled, "Momma," knowing it was the proverbial standoff, that neither one of us would budge until finally I reached out to her and said, "I forgot something upstairs, want to walk back up with me?" as if nothing were wrong, and she flashed a smile and said, "Beam me up, Scotty!" and that's what happened three years later when he did... he beamed her up, "Force field down, equal with her father at last, assimilation complete. (635)

Oh What a Brute-of-a Morning!
(A true story)
by Diane H. Larson

I WAS DEEPLY IMMERSED IN ONE of the most nourishing dreams I'd had in years, being seen and heard in such a profound way that I wanted more, when the alarm beeped me awake, allowing no time for me to savor my incredible dream or to cuddle my wee dog Bertie who, when he hears me stir in the morning, crawls under the covers for our special snuggle, but I needed to stop for gas to drive the longer-than-usual distance to my once-a-month Women's Circle, so I jumped out of bed, pulled off my PJs and was just heading to the shower when I noticed that Himself had forgotten to turn off the air cleaner, so I grumpily hauled my nude body around to his side of the bed to take care of it, in the process stepping smack-dab in a puddle of dog vomit on the rug, which shocked me, since during the night, after hearing Bertie gagging, I asked Himself to check the rug, and he did, reporting that there was "nothing there"... well obviously something WAS there... and taking my life in my hands, I called him away from his morning coffee to come and clean up the mess and put the rug in the laundry basket, after which I remembered that the rug would need to soak before I washed it, so I went to take care of it, and a good thing I did, as pieces of vomited dog food still clung to the rug, and I had to scrape the mess off with my fingernails before putting the rug in to soak, so it was only after that, when I finally climbed into the tub and started to turn on the shower, that I discovered that the hot water heater installer, who is also a plumber, when checking out our shower faucet for a possible leak the previous day, which he thought might have caused the new hot water tank to leak on the day after it was installed, resulting in the new leak alarm going off in the middle of the night, and thank goodness it did, or we might have awakened to a watery mess, though don't ask me why the installer had to check for a leak in the shower, as I couldn't possibly explain it to you, even after he explained it to me six times, must not have screwed the faucet in tightly, because it fell off in my hand, making it seem even more likely that the REAL reason the water heater leaked was because the installer didn't screw the pipes in tightly on the water heater either, necessitating me calling Himself to come and fix the faucet in order for me to shower, but he couldn't figure out how to get the face off the faucet handle, though I reminded him that he had done it many times, but of course he didn't like hearing that, so I figured out how to do it myself, after which, while he was tightening the faucet, he just happened to mention that he had noticed the night before when he was bathing the dog that the faucet was loose, and naturally, which I'm absolutely positive ANY normal person would have done under similar circumstances, I asked him why the hell he hadn't fixed it THEN, irritating him such that he snarled at me before stomping back to his coffee, and therefore, I'm quite certain that he was none too happy when, after my shower, I interrupted him for a third time to come and rub cream on my back, as he does this daily, which is truly so sweet of him, though neither of us felt at all sweet that morning... more like two old crabs, claws out, swinging at one another... oh what a brute-of-a morning! (637)

My Real-life Miracle!
by Doris Hughes Green

I DIDN'T KNOW HE WAS A SPECIAL NEEDS CHILD until nine months after he was born when I found out something was wrong with my baby because he wasn't sitting up, and as a young mother with her first child, I didn't know what to expect, when a group of Jehovah Witnesses stopped by my house to offer a Bible Study with me, and I accepted, and soon they noticed Carlos' behavior and insisted I take him to the doctor, which I did, only to find out, he was born brain-damaged, diagnosed as cerebral palsy, and as a young single woman who just moved from Mississippi, uneducated and green, I became a heartbroken mommy who had just discovered her baby wasn't like most babies, but I knew God had sent those Witnesses to my door to save me from doing something stupid, although it took time for me to accept Carlos' diagnosis and accept the fact that he would need my care for the rest of his life, but I soon learned that being the mother of a special needs child requires a lot of work because I have to do everything for him and he loves me dearly for taking care of him, especially when people come around and can see through Carlos' loud sounds that say he's happy, his mother takes care of him and keeps him safe, something that creates a special spiritual connection, which resulted in a miracle back in April 2012, Easter Sunday, when God healed Carlos at the age of 32, and he spoke a complete sentence for the first time ever, a miracle from my God because up to that time he had only answered any of my questions with "I don't know", so it took a few minutes to realize I had heard his sweet voice speak for the first time, which changed my life, causing me to realize that Carlos is part of my ministry to show the world the real love of God, and when I heard his voice for the first time, I went to praising God for healing my baby (I call Carlos, *my baby* because I take care of him like a baby) just as Jesus did when he walked the earth healing the blind and raising the dead, and after all these years, he's talking more so that when I say, "I love you Carlos," he whispers back in my ear, "I love you," and it sounds like he sings it to me, yet I hear him clearly and it melts my heart every time, because I know that one day he will speak clearly and hold a conversation with me and that would make me oh so happy, just knowing why God gave him to me, which has resulted in giving me a mission to change the world into a happy place through such things as my radio ministry, emphasizing weekly my message of "New Beginnings", and the company I founded and serve as CEO — Divine Divas Ministries, LLC — composed of women on a mission to change this world, helping others to know the real love of God (men are welcome to work with us too) and I know when Carlos converses, it will change lives because I know how it feels when he speaks some sentences and sounds, like when he told me once at church that something was bothering him, and my fellow parishioners prayed for him and the next day, he said, "Mom," and he's been calling me Mom, ever since, something that surprised me and I love to hear him call me Mom for it took him many years to get out that one word, so "Wow!" I know that once God performs a miracle, more miracles are coming and Carlos, now 37, is my gift from God and the love of my life. (643)

Just Like Rabbits
by Suezy Proctor

VISUALIZE AN ANT HILL, the kind that dominates your parking strip and every corner of your yard, then visualize what happens when you give it a good swift kick, causing ants to spew out like lava flowing from an erupting volcano, which has me wondering how many ants there are in an ant hill — statistics say there are more bugs in one square acre of ground than humans on the planet — but I'm not going to talk about ants today, no, I am going to talk about rabbits, because counting rabbits in southeastern Idaho and northeastern Nevada is like counting ants in an area the size of the state of Vermont, and where Idaho and Nevada meet on an eastern corner that once was an unbroken sage-brush plain, it is estimated that as many as 900,000 jack rabbits inhabit this area in any given year, and just so you know, rabbit drives have been a part of farming in the West for more than 150 years, with early records reporting more than 400,000 rabbits killed in one year alone, and where eventually, all across the West, annual rabbit drives were held on Thanksgiving morning, and this is how the jack rabbit became the new Thanksgiving turkey, and all of this was brought to life for me in 1981 when I set out from Washington state and headed for Las Vegas, Nevada, in my 1974 Triumph Spitfire Convertible, with the top down, making good time the first day and reaching Jackpot, Nevada — the first gambling town inside the Nevada border just south of Twin Falls Idaho — at dusk, and since I was hungry, I pulled into Cactus Pete's Casino & Steakhouse for dinner, and by the time I finished, it was dark and it was hot — 108 degrees — when I hopped back into my car and headed south on Highway

93, a virtual straight shot to Las Vegas... about a seven-hour drive, and by the time I'd reach Las Vegas it would be a record-breaking 128 degrees, but as I approached the edge of town, a glowing billboard assured me there were no services for another 212 miles, no lights, no rest stops, no nuthin', 'ceptin' ginormous jack rabbits that literally covered every inch of the road so they could soak up the stored heat in the asphalt, and I remember this well because my car had a whoppin' five inches of clearance from the road... five measly inches, whereby sitting in the driver's seat, I could look those jack rabbits in the eye if they were sitting up, although some of them of course were smaller, but many, as they sat, were sitting taller than I sat in the seat of my car, and I didn't want to hit any of them, so for a while, I drove about four to five miles an hour, beeping my horn as I went, and when after fifteen minutes of that, a huge triple-trailer semi-truck whizzed past me doing about 95 miles an hour, and OH! The Carnage! and I had to gain my composure to put on the gas and catch up with the truck to drive behind it as long as I could, so it could take the hits, because hitting any jack rabbit would seriously and very expensively damage my car... and all this, as if in a flashback, because on my return home a few months later, I drove through the same area in the daylight and came upon "The Great Jack Rabbit Roundup of 1981", as it is remembered today, where 400 farmers on horseback, motorcycles, and on foot, armed with real and make-shift weapons gathered to eliminate hundreds of thousands of jack rabbits, and I ask you to remember the ant hill... what happens to it when you treat it with chemicals... it disappears and another ant hill pops up some place nearby, just like rabbits! (650)

Like He Didn't Know...
by Donna Lee Anderson

I THOUGHT I WAS BEING FUNNY but it seems no one else got it when I poured my drink all over his stupid head, and even that didn't stop him from laughing and saying un-truths about his prowess and the smooth moves he thinks he possesses just because young women smile when he cracks a joke about their various body parts, saying things like "cute jiggle in the back of that buggy when you walk" and "presenting a pretty nice front there, honey", and he doesn't seem to get that now that he is married, yes to me, that this is embarrassing for me when he flirts, and especially when he makes a point of going to their table and chatting and sometimes coming back to me and tucking his notebook back into his inside jacket pocket thinking he is hiding it from me, and like I don't know he gathers phone numbers and quite often calls these honeys and meets up with them, like I don't know he is using the line about being a talent scout, and like he thinks I won't tell these honeys he is a liar and hasn't worked since he got his inheritance from his mother, and now, since it is getting late — almost 1:00 a.m. — and we are headed home and he is still laughing and reliving his so-called contacts tonight, and actually expecting me to join in on his charming meetings while I'm busy thinking of how I can get out of this marriage and away from this idiot, and then reality sets in that I don't have any money of my own because I haven't worked for over a year, and even though he set me up with my own check book, I still have to wait for his deposits to that account every month and even though I have been socking away money I only have about ten thousand dollars and that won't go very far if I have to pay rent and buy all my food and gas and insurance, so I needed to think about how to make this pay for me, some way to show him what a jerk he is, how unhappy I am, and whether or not this could be fixed, this marriage I mean, or if it can't, how much money could I expect to come to me, so I bring up the subject of "maybe this union should be cancelled," and he says "hell no, I like our arrangement," and I ask "did it matter that I wasn't happy," and he answers "not really, as long as I kept a clean house and did the wifely thing in the bedroom when needed" and that's when the plan came into being (it wouldn't take very much planning since he was pretty drunk), with the result that when we pulled into the garage, I asked if he could just leave the car running for a few minutes with the head lights on so I could get that box with the picture frames that we stored there so I could put up some of my kids pictures, and he said okay, and as I moved around the garage looking for the right box, he closed the garage door and I could see him relaxing and putting his head back and so when I eased out of the garage's side door, went around to the front door and let myself in, I could still hear the car running, but I just went upstairs to the bedroom, got undressed and took a shower and yes, I could still hear the motor of the car, but maybe he went to sleep, and that would be okay with me, make my plan easier if he sat in that garage with the car running all night, then I could explain to the authorities that we were fighting and when we got home I got out and came in and he said he'd be in as soon as he cooled down, but guess he fell asleep and now he's not going to wake up but, that's the breaks, and now all that inheritance is mine too, and I knew I'd figure out a way to solve this problem. (706)

The Easy Choices
by Leslie Crane

FOLLOWING THE DEATH OF MY BROTHER I needed to get away and my one and only sister had moved to Montana, so it was an easy choice to visit her, which turned out to be two short flights on United Express in which the first flight took me to Spokane and from there flew me into Montana, but the first flight was to become my "most embarrassing moment" because after drinking many cups of coffee, some of which were offered at the gate by United, I discovered too late that there was no toilet on the aircraft that was smaller than most and, I know it seems almost unbelievable but this was 1990 when the passengers actually had to walk out onto the tarmac and climb stairs to board the plane, where there were two rows of two seats and, for some unknown reason, the carpet appeared to cover a shape similar to a 2 x 4 between my seat and the two men directly across from me, so I waited for the plane to hit the desired altitude and when the "buckle your seat belt" light went out I unbuckled my seat belt, stood up, and walked to the back of the plane, and that's when I discovered that there wasn't a bathroom, so the two guys across from me who knew what was going on suggested that I speak to the pilot (because there wasn't a steward/stewardess) who informed me of our ETA, and I informed him that there was no possible way that I could hold it, which made him a bit uncomfortable, and in addition his co-pilot pretended to be completely absorbed in what he was doing and ignored his pleading glances, so the pilot suggested that I take a barf bag and go to the back of the plane and pee in it, and when I returned to my seat, I shared my dilemma with my two neighbors and gave a quick thought to my choices, realizing the barf bag was the better of the two options, so I looked around to check out the area at the back of the plane and noticed an older gentleman who was sitting too close to the back of the plane and, fortunately the plane wasn't full, so I asked him politely if he would please move forward a couple seats, without providing any reason, and he kindly accommodated my request, which was a huge relief, so I borrowed my neighbors large coat, grabbed my barf bag and headed to the rear of the plane while thinking to myself that I would NEVER see these people again, which helped me endure this humiliation as I spread the large coat across the two back seats, set down my barf bag with the opening as wide as I could make it, then, while holding my jacket over the empty space below the large coat, I wiggled out of my jeans and peed and peed and peed and it felt like I could have filled up a gallon jug, but we all know that women can't aim and I was no exception because, although I did fill up the barf bag three-quarters of the way, the rest trailed down the aisle and stopped when it hit the 2 x 4 bump between me and my two neighbors, whereby I quickly pulled up my jeans, folded the barf bag, set it by the door, and went back to my seat after returning the coat, so you can imagine how entertained my two new "friends" were, but when I told them to look at the carpet and they saw the trail of urine, they laughed very hard and very loud, and when we landed and the pilot instructed us to watch our step when we disembarked, they yelled, "You ain't a-kiddin, watch your step," and even though they were laughing at me, I couldn't really blame them because even the older gentleman who I had asked to move forward a couple of seats couldn't contain himself when he saw that I was on his connecting flight, so the good news is, that after all these years the memory has faded a bit and I don't know any of the people that were on that plane, but from that day forward, I do know ahead of time if and where there is a bathroom, because one tends to get a tad bit paranoid after an experience like that. (745)

pocket sized scythe
by holly woodie

tolerating boorish death as he stands with his cloak in his outstretched hand and says wash this for me and i return you want i should bleach it and he laughs head back saying try it and i will kill thee just get the travel dust off as i say i will have to go to the laundromat since my machine is not big enough and he says i will make them go away for a short time anyway as he waves his crooked hands laughing again though i cannot say why while he takes a seat in the comfy chair saying this is where i will stay until you get back and i ask do you have any quarters to which he shakes his head and laughs saying drachmas though i dont expect they will accept that and i stuff the cloak in the washer where it gleams dull as it moves by itself and it is so dirty i could walk away but i will do as he asks because who wants to upset death himself until finally out of the wash it is heavy as hell and i bring over a rolling basket just to move it to the drier at seven minutes per quarter that will take a ten spot when it finally dries and i take it back home in the car taking it slow so i wont get in a wreck not wanting him to collect the cloak and myself in the same jump and as i hand it over folded nicely he takes it shakes it no more travel dust just hints of dark light and the occasional moving face as he dons his clean cloak looking regal and deadly a force of nature forever testing me and he asks are you ready to come with me as i chuckle out of the side of my mouth and ask are you serious and he replies yes but to be my apprentice for i cannot hold this mantel indefinitely and i ask what would you have me do die and become you and he says yes of sorts and i ask i have a choice to which of course he replies we all choose where we go in life and i ask so as in death how long will i live dead as long as you see fit he says why me i ask because when i came you were not afraid you have a stout heart that will not break as you take the life of others leading them on their way oh i say will it be forever yes he says until you find an apprentice yourself it will be sad i say he says do not think of it that way it is the last step in a life lived well or not your job would be to lead them not to drop them off as the boatmen do that heaven hell purgatory nirvana the pit or reborn on earth depending on their beliefs there is a place for all he says is it fulfilling work i ask yes he says with your kind face and i ask will my face change to resemble yours gnarled and overly deadly he says it will be as you wish if you take the cloak and i say i would prefer to look the same and he says of course you would it is in your dna do i have time to think about it he says no you must decide today what will happen to you i ask i will go to elysium for all my good hard work when your training is complete just because i look this way does not mean i died in a bad way i just stayed too long on the trail without an apprentice life force i am not bad just misunderstood he concludes i wrestle in my mind with living longer and doing lifes work or stopping time to become deaths guide and finally i say yes yes i will take the apprentices cloak because it will be the best way to take care of others soothing them in their last moments when only they can see and hear me i will become lady death just as you wish but for myself to help this is the best way i can think of with my heart and head to live well and ask do i have to carry a scythe to which he replies it is your choice you could carry a pocket-sized a less fearsome version of the tool of the trade okay i say i will do that and bowing he presents me with the apprentices cloak and says thank you and you will not regret this he says adding little one you look good in black (802)

Alley People
by Sara Jacobelli

October 1st, 1970

D<small>EAR</small> D<small>IARY</small>: M<small>OM BOUGHT ME THIS DIARY</small> for my birthday so I'm going to write about my life and the way I spend a lot of time looking out of my second floor window to the alley next to our apartment building and, on the other side of the alley is a bar and pizza parlor, and I've seen kids fight and play in that alley and smoke cigarettes and in the summer slide down it on big pieces of cardboard and light firecrackers and yell with delight when they went off, and in the winter they throw snowballs at each other and shriek and laugh red-faced and puff out their cheeks to blow out cold clouds of air that float away, and at night-time I hear the jukebox from the bar, the jukebox that wails with sad songs and happy songs, and I smell the garlic and mozzarella on the pizza, and see so much, such as I've seen men pee in the alley, I've seen women drop their purses and bend down to pick up change, I've seen gossiping high school girls put on make-up and fix their hair, I've seen young lovers making out with all those tender whispers and giggles, I've seen couples my parents' age arguing as the men yell and the women cry, I've seen teenagers who drank too much get sick, and I've seen them smoke weed and heard them cough, and I've seen people buying drugs, and I saw a man get robbed at gunpoint by another man when I thought I was going to witness a murder — not for the first time — but the second man gave up his wallet to the first man who held a gun on him and I held my breath, for what I don't know, thinking that this window I look out of is like a TV because sometimes it feels like what's happening outside my window isn't real, only what's happening inside here is real, but I gotta admit when dinner's done, I don't want to stay in the living room and watch TV and play games with my brothers and sister and my two cousins who live with us (because their mom's a drunk, not nice like our mom), instead I want to go back to my bedroom and look out the window, even though Mom says I'm too nosey and she laughs and says, "You remind me of Jimmy Stewart in that movie 'Rear Window'," and she says I should watch it, adding that the Jimmy Stewart character is in a wheelie chair, like me, looking out the window all day, but it's one of those old-timey black and white movies she loves so much, and she says, "I'm sorry the neighborhood's got so bad, but that's why I've gotta keep all you kids inside," and we haven't been outside in two years, three months, seventeen days — not to school or to church or the store or the laundromat or the Girl's Club or the Boy's Club or the beach in the summer or to jump into big piles of leaves in the fall or to go trick or treating at Halloween or to go to Aunt Ruthie's for Thanksgiving dinner when her apartment fills up with the delicious smell of turkey and stuffing and pumpkin pie with whipped cream — or to drive around and see Christmas lights in the winter — and that's because ever since me and my brother got shot walking home from school by some teenagers in the Diamond Heights Gang, and Gino died — my brown-curly-haired big brother who all the girls had crushes on, he died on the sidewalk right in front of me and I ended up in a wheelie chair — and I'm so sad he's gone, but I can zoom around the apartment pretty fast in my chair and Mom said we're never going outside again, not if she can help it, so she goes to work and the grocery store and the laundromat all by herself and we stay here, knowing this is our world now, just Mom and all us kids cuz Poppy left, saying he "couldn't take it anymore," and she says there's guns and knives and gangs and drugs out there, and in here we have TV and the radio and hot chocolate and popcorn and it's cool in the summer and warm and cozy in the winter and she said, "I want to keep you kids safe," and "I want to keep you kids alive," and sometimes I want to scream out my window, "Look at me, World, My name is Victoria but everyone calls me Tori, I'm thirteen years old, here I am, World!", but I never do that, so while the other kids watch TV and play Sorry! and Crazy Eights and Scrabble and Life and boring never-ending games of Monopoly, I look out my window and watch the Alley People living their lives, their long long long complicated tragic sad happy amazing mysterious beautiful lives. (840)

Lida Rose
by Kenny Gordon

Lida Rose was a flirt, which is something that everyone knew and talked about, like when she stepped out with a fellow who was selling magazine subscriptions or vacuum cleaners door-to-door and kept her door open to him for all the time he was in town, but when he left she changed her tune and took to fancying another feller named Jake who had been hanging around her, like all the other fellers in town, but Jake had more on his mind than just stepping out with her, but unfortunately his ideas stayed in his head for Jake was about as shy as anybody could be, and especially those guys around Lida Rose, for she flirted outrageously until one of those guys made a move toward her and then she turned her back and froze him out while she continued to flirt with some other rascal until along came that slick salesman, back in town after a couple of months, and of course he headed straight for Lida Rose's doorway, which opened to welcome him back, and they were next seen dancing at Bob's Poolroom and Saloon Emporium, dancing those new-fangled dances that put naughty ideas in the heads of anyone near the dance floor, but especially in the heads of the dancers, and that salesman was no different, grinning a special salesman's grin as if he was just about to close the most important and financially advantageous deal in all of sales history, and which only caused Lida Rose to dance more energetically, twistin' and gyratin' like a kind of snake about to devour its prey... until the music stopped, dead quiet, and a solemn looking preacher arose from the shadows and faced the dancers and, in fact, the whole emporium, causing the pool players to lay down their cues, the imbibers in the saloon to swallow the last liquid from their mugs quickly so as not to lose a drop because they knew what the preacher was about to say for they had heard it before, whenever the old dude got upset with his wife or couldn't come up with a new sermon topic (for he had run out of sins to preach against) or when he had an upset stomach and wanted to blame it all on the sinful world around him (and not on the whiskey bottle hidden in the back of his desk drawer), and this night was no different for the preacher had spread a heavy hush across the emporium as he focused his gaze on Lida Rose and her dance partner, frozen amid one of their fancier steps, her arms entwined about his neck, clinging to him so she wouldn't lose her balance, and he clinging to her, arms where they probably shouldn't have been, although Lida Rose didn't object, until the preacher raised his arms, both of them, in mid-air and in the most stentorian (don't you love that word: sten-tor-ian!) voice pronounced the world had gone to hell overnight to allow the goings-on that he was witnessing, never mind that no one else thought they were going to hell, and that he, Mr. Preacherman, was there to save their doomed souls from perdition (another lovely word) if only the souls gathered around him would give up their "lewd and lascivious" activity and join him in falling to their knees to pray for their salvation… and that's when the door opened and in walked Jake, shy Jake, quiet Jake, never-talk-out-of-turn Jake, but this time he wasn't quiet or shy and he was ready to talk, looking straight at the preacher and giving him the what-ho about interrupting people enjoying a night of fun, people letting their hair down, and people who he didn't even know, and scaring the daylights out of some who weren't acquainted with the yelping preacherman, rather than keeping his opinions to himself and returning immediately to his sheltered dull, dreary, and deadly life where he had forgotten the feeling of joy or the idea of happiness or that he had given up on the beauty of hope and love of life, and when he was finished admonishing the once-noisy preacher, Jake walked straight over to Lida Rose, took her hand, and asked the band to begin playing another tune so they could dance, which is what they did, but

not just for that evening, but for many evenings to come, many, many, many… swaying to the dance over and over as Jake sang his song to Lida Rose, humming first then singing:
Lida Rose, I'm home again, Rose,
To get the sun back in the sky,
Lida Rose, I'm home again, Rose,
About a thousand kisses shy,
Ding dong ding
I can hear the chapel bell chime,
Ding dong ding
At the least suggestion I'll pop the question,
Lida Rose, I'm home again, Rose,
Without a sweetheart to my name,
Lida Rose, now everyone knows
That I am hoping you're the same
So here is my love song, not fancy or fine,
Lida Rose, oh won't you be mine,
Lida Rose, oh Lida Rose, oh Lida Rose… (850)

My Careers
by Jim Teeters

CAREER SUCCESS FORMS A LARGE PART of how we view our personal worth and if I am riding high in my work life, making money, using my talents and regularly enjoying the admiration of my superiors and fellow workers, I feel like an able and worthy person and that's a nice place to be, and though I hold my head high in other life spheres such as my home, my friends, community groups or church, I find that failure in my careers is viewed as personal failure, which often results in social rejection and ostracism (banishment from normal societal intercourse), one of the ancient community rituals we allegedly gave up long ago but is still operating in our cyberspace-age society as we almost daily look right past countless numbers of people on the streets of our cities who roam about, relegated to shameful poverty having failed the means test of personal worth, thus remain powerless because they have not scored success in the world of work, so this is today's banishment and the rest of us keep trying hard to impress anyone we can of our accomplishments, real or made up, which is good for the ego but not so good for the soul as Jesus once said, "For what is a man profited, if he shall gain the whole world, and lose his own soul," but success of the soul is not as popular these days and even less visible, so to prove our worth we make every effort at getting and giving status based on career accomplishments — these being both popular and visible — and I am not immune to these pressures but I have become brutally honest about my failings in my careers, where others would hide embarrassing facts and avoid rejection, however, I will lay out before you the bitter truth and, who knows, perhaps my sacrifice will help me build a healthy spirit and I ask that your judgments, dear reader, like a refining fire, will purify my soul as I recount for you the following: my first real, career-related job started at the Sound-View Branch of the YMCA in Seattle where I was hired as a youth program director and within three-and-a-half years that branch closed for lack of memberships, so I escaped to the Graduate School of Social Work at the University of Hawaii after getting married (my marriage is a success story, which will have to be told in another essay on that subject) so…

…next, I launched my graduate social work career as a therapist at Madison County Family Services in Indiana and three years later the client load fell off, the director quit, and after suffering an ulcer from my role as Acting Director, I left for Oregon country to teach social work in a small western college…

…where my career as a college professor ended abruptly after a few years when the college failed financially and closed its doors permanently and this began a painful period of unemployment which lasted until…

…my next job, in staff development, with the State of Oregon, that lasted quite a while and I did not witness the demise of the Oregon State Government, but the Staff Development Section in my department was decimated suddenly and again I escaped, just in time, to follow my spiritual calling as a church pastor, believing that surely, God's work would be secure, I figured, but…

…the church I worked for as associate pastor lost two lead pastors, so I tried to hang on, but because of church protocol that lead pastors should work with a clean staff slate, I had to vacate before the third one showed up, and thus…

…I went to Kent, Washington, where I took over as head pastor of a shaky little Quaker congregation and I performed ecclesiastical CPR over the next four years, but the church's vital organs did not respond, and following my resignation, the church closed; therefore, it was time to start my own business, I reasoned…

…and I was a good speaker and trainer, so I organized a seminar business and we nearly lost our home from this unwise scheme, and after the collapse of Creative Seminars, my nephew Brian (a very successful Naval officer), came to visit us and he'd been writing some notes and was running out of our scratch paper when he sarcastically quipped, "Uncle Jim, I'm out of scratch paper, so I'll just use some of your failed-business brochures," and I assented but admitted it kind of stung, but my wife, bless her, wanting to boost my morale, suggested I should hire myself out as a secret weapon to corporations facing tough competition and get a job with their competitors and that might work for advancing my soul… and next… maybe I'll write a book…

…because, as of revising this piece into the one-sentence format, I successfully completed seventeen years working in a healthy Washington State bureaucracy and ran a nice little writing and training business out of my home, published many books, and now I'm retired at age 79 and I feel pretty happy with my life and rarely complain! (856)

Bruce the Plumber
by Kathy Wilson

He was peering intently at me with squinty eyes, moving his face closer and closer to mine until I could feel his warm breath on my cheeks, and then just when I was deciding if I wanted to step backward and away from him or to move in closer to feel the texture of his lush lips, his eyes suddenly went all big and round as he quickly shifted backward, standing erect and yet continuing to stare at me with an almost scary intensity until finally he blurted out, "You're Kathy the Roofer," making me giggle with relief that he wasn't thinking of performing some exciting yet scary act such as kissing me, but was instead merely recognizing me as the locally famous and sometimes notorious woman roofer who for five years had drawn the attention of males of all ages who were involved in the many facets of the residential construction industry in and around the small rural area in which I lived and worked on Washington's Olympic Peninsula, at a time when my current admirer, Bruce, who was still standing in front of me beaming with delight at his discovery of my identity, had been a teenager working for his step-dad Paul in his plumbing business, a job he sort of fell into after his mother divorced her first husband, Bruce's father, because he was always out of town, on the road traveling from town to town and bar to bar, where he and his very small Western band, consisting of a drummer, a base guitarist, and Bruce's dad as lead singer and steel guitarist, played their brand of twangy music and whined on in the nasally male voices heard only in Country Western songs which seem to be interminably about losing their woman, dog, horse, and/or truck, but never their cows, which I always found odd since they were supposed to be *cow*-boys, always playing to a new audience, or so it seemed, since their gigs moved farther and farther away from home, meaning Bruce's birth dad was gone for longer and longer periods of time, until finally his mother Mae couldn't take the loneliness anymore and began an affair with her husband's live-in war buddy, Paul, whom he had met and befriended in a military hospital in Germany where both men had been taken after suffering injuries from gunfire during a battle, after which Paul had moved from his native country of Germany to live with Bruce's dad and mom, hoping to find his version of the American Dream, since the work opportunities in post-war Germany were mostly cleaning up the debris of war, which paid very little, so with the support of his American buddy, Paul found that he had a knack for all things mechanical and a specific talent for plumbing, which led him to start his business, where he developed a loyal following among the local contractors who appreciated his Germanic trait of engineering efficiency and perfection as it applied to the plumbing in the houses they built, so that eventually his business grew to the point that he needed help, and where better to find his work crew than within his own family, even if they were at that time unofficial family, but as things continued to heat up between him and Mae, it was pretty obvious that there was one too many men in the house and one of them would have to go, which wasn't such a difficult decision to make for anyone involved in the triangle of Bruce's birth dad, his mom, and Paul, since one of the men was pretty much absent already, what with his musical career taking him farther and farther away, reducing his time at home with his wife until it was almost never, so it was no big surprise to Bruce when he came home from high school one day to find the doors to the house locked and a lot of moaning, groaning, bed springs squeaking, and other such sounds coming from his mom's bedroom, an occurrence which became more commonplace as Mae and Paul intensified their relationship to become more than just friends, until one day they finally held a family conference, sans Bruce's father who was off who-knew-where with his band, and told Bruce that his mom and dad were getting divorced so that Paul and Mae could get married and he would then have a new father, which was not much in the way of news to Bruce since for at least a couple of years Paul had slowly and steadily been taking the position of male head of the household, including beginning to teach Bruce about plumbing, and that was when Bruce came to know me as Kathy the Roofer, at a time when he was working with his step-dad on the rough-in portion of the plumbing on a house being built while I was on the roof, banging away as I installed some sort of roofing material, and as I did so, drawing the admiring stares of a teenage boy who had never seen a woman working in construction, especially in the roofing profession which is extremely demanding physically, an experience for the young and impressionable teenager which forever changed his inner vision of women from that of only housewives, mothers, secretaries, and the like, to a new vision, one that opened his awareness so that he began to appreciate women for their strength, both inner and physical, their endurance, their adaptability, and all the other capabilities that enable and allow them to become as adept at any job, any type of work, that a man can perform. (941)

Me Too, Gotcha!
by Ruth Anderson

NINE WOMEN OF ASSORTED AGES, sizes, capabilities, and temperament filed into the attractive board room of OpNow Incorporated (a large Seattle trading firm that had become the "go-to place" for smaller companies wishing to do business with Asian interests), each woman holding an impressive position in the company, the meeting having been called by the senior woman present, Chief Financial Officer (CFO) Tabitha Clawson, a statuesque woman of forty-two, with bleached blond hair, darting brown eyes, and the annoying habit of crossing her arms under her ample breasts and lifting them up when she was dissatisfied with an answer, which seemed to those who worked closely with her to be rather more often than was called for, and with mounting curiosity and some trepidation, the women seated themselves, placed their cell phones on the table, as was the habit of the company executives for crucial meetings, this being one for sure, though having only women present did give the room a very different air, in more ways than one, and so the CFO seated herself at the head of the long, handsome table and, drawing a deep breath, laid out the issue, to wit that OpNow was the only sizeable company in Seattle, maybe on the West Coast, that had not yet divulged the names of any male colleagues who had sexually harassed women colleagues, and it was simply believed it could not be the case that none of the women present had been the subject of such unwanted attention as large as the company was and as many men as worked there, for goodness sake, for which oversight the women at the table would not be leaving until one or more had revealed incidents of harassment that could take down at least one of their male colleagues, and it had to be someone fairly important whose name would eventually be given to Poppy Travers, the evening desk reporter of a local television station, who was waiting to hear whom OpNow would "out," at which point, Eun Keith, head of Human Resources, a petite, thoroughly professional Korean-American woman in her 50s, rose from the table and, in a controlled voice announced that no complaints of this nature had recently reached her office and she wouldn't participate in this witch hunt, which everyone knew meant she wouldn't do what Tabitha wanted no matter what it was, the two of them having been at odds for years, and Eun departed, followed by three other women whom Tabitha had no purview over, leaving five women to decide the fate of one of their male colleagues, but despite Tabitha standing and parading in front of them, begging them to speak, an uneasy silence was maintained until one of the women mentioned Drew Nolan, the top sales rep in the marketing department, a man of sixty-six, who had been higher up in the company at one time, but who enjoyed sales and had asked to revert to a non-managerial post pending retirement, and who had always championed women co-workers because he liked their company, and for the most part their work ethic, and his way of showing his pleasure with them was to pat them on the back, or occasionally a knee, but his desk full of pictures of his wife, kids, and grandkids, about whom he frequently told stories, had other women at the table shaking their heads in disbelief, and as it dawned on them that this jovial, helpful colleague might appear on the evening news because he had sexually harassed one or more of them, women began to shift in their seats, and two more left, prompting Tabitha to curse, cross her arms beneath her breasts and announce to the two remaining younger women that they would tell OpNow Chief Executive Officer Brad Folger that Drew Nolan had harassed them, and she ended the meeting by storming out the door, leaving the two apprehensive women to take their complaints against Nolan to Folger, who subsequently called in his Chief

Operating Officer, Li Ho, as well as Eun Keith, and others and, armed with results of the not-too-surprising discussion, Folger called a special board meeting, following which, two days hence, he summoned Tabitha, Ho, and Keith, and told Tabitha that he knew she was in search of a sexual predator and "luckily" they had one to offer, for he had done some research also and had learned that Tabitha herself had sexually harassed a male subordinate during a business trip to Singapore, showing up scantily clothed at his hotel room late at night, intimating if he didn't let her in, he'd lose his job, and two Asian businessmen had complained that she seemed to wear unnecessarily revealing clothes in their presence, and so it appeared that OpNow had found the harasser whom Tabitha was looking for, and the male subordinate had taken photos that had come to light and would compromise her should she be inclined to sue, so would she please take the severance package Folger pointed to on his desk in lieu of a call to Poppy Travers (who would in any event eagerly report the outcome several days hence, causing a major stir among media outlets), which led the fuming, red-faced CFO to grab the package, and head for the door followed by Ho who escorted her out of the building and down to her car where she found her coat and other personal items in a box sitting on the trunk with a note on top from Eun Keith containing a list of pertinent job openings — in San Francisco — and a notice that Drew Nolan had, that day, put in his retirement papers. (945)

Lookie, Cookie
by Val Dumond

L̲ittle Shirley was the smallest and youngest in her tap dancing class, only five years old (named after the famous movie star Shirley Temple), considered "cute" but certainly not beautiful, she left that to her best friend Joyce whose blond curly hair and slim seven-year-old body resembled more today's Olympic gymnasts, while Shirley suffered with straight brown hair that resisted attempts of curling irons as forcefully as the girl herself resisted what they used to call "showing off" (one of Joyce's best traits), for they lived kitty corner from each other and had become best friends, spending hours at Joyce's home above her father's cheese factory that turned out to provide Shirley with a deep lifelong appreciation for good (aged) cheese, so when Joyce's mother convinced Shirley's mother that the girls would have fun in the new tap dancing class, Shirley began regular Saturday morning lessons, which amused Madame Provinska because the little girl had the beat and could memorize the routines but she had no style, apparently something very important for dancers, and soon Shirley was having a good time, especially since her mother became the piano *acompanist* for the troupe, giving Shirley one-on-one time with Mom, away from her baby sister, until summer arrived and the Saturday trips became monotonous until the day Madame Provinska announced to her young dancers that they would be featured at the Fourth of July Town Celebration, even getting to ride in the parade, and Shirley and Joyce huddled together to plan their special day, that turned out almost sunny, beginning with the parade as the girls either jumped up on or were lifted up to the large flatbed truck that usually hauled cabbage from the fields to the sauerkraut factory, which employed most of the men and boys in town either in the fields or the factory, but which was holiday decorated that day with red, white, and blue balloons and streamers for the town dancers, now decked out in pink crepe paper dresses with bows on their ankles and wrists, who posed as the flatbed took its place in line and began the journey from the high school yard down Main Street, past the Methodist Church and the sauerkraut factory, and into the town park at the end of the main drag where the girls were set up in a place where they could see the glistening waters of the lake through the trees, under which the women were already spreading their table cloths and placing rows of potluck dishes of hot dogs, fried chicken, cole slaw, potato salad, green Jell-O salad, and sauerkraut of course, along with pickles, olives, and nuts, and ending up with an entire picnic table full of cakes and pies that awaited the ice cream being churned by some young boys who the older dancers recognized and began to tease as the younger girls watched and wondered why they bothered to even notice the boys, some even smiling weirdly at them and gesturing their outstretched arms as the boys pretended not to notice, but they did, whispering among themselves as their weary arms turned and churned the developing ice cream until one of the men announced grandly (Joyce told Shirley he was the mayor) that the meal would begin with grace pronounced by the pastor of the Methodist Church, after which lines of hungry townspeople formed at the tables where the food soon disappeared onto plates that rested where each family had spread out their own tables or blankets to enjoy the bountiful feast, after which a few lay back for a brief afternoon nap before the show began, scheduled for three o'clock, at which time the dancers' mothers hastily began to remove spots and creases in the pink crepe paper dresses, comb their daughters' hair, and wipe faces covered with mustard, green Jell-O, chocolate cake and ice cream before reminding them not to watch their feet and to keep smiling as they danced, so that when the announcement was made over the loud-speaker that the program would be led off by Madam Provinska's dancing troupe, the girls hurried to the flatbed truck and climbed up hastily provided steps and waited for Shirley's mother to play the opening strains of their music before they marched provocatively onto the "stage" making circles with their arms as they tapped their routine and sang, "*Lookie, lookie, lookie / here comes Cookie, walking down the street / lookie, lookie, lookie / here comes Cookie, ain't she sweet?*" at which moment the men who had gathered around the flatbed whistled and shouted words that Shirley couldn't understand as the boys, some barely poking their heads above the flatbed surface, clapped their hands and copied the whistles of the men and shot leering smiles at the girls, who tried to maintain the smiles pasted on their faces, but it wasn't easy, for they were feeling disdain probably for the first time and they were not delighted, although to their credit, they remembered their dance steps and managed to ignore, as much as possible, the yells and jeers they were experiencing, and afterward, as they tried to climb down from the flatbed, the older girls were almost knocked off their young legs as a couple of the men attempted to hug them, but Madame Provinska immediately came to their rescue and guided her troupe back to their families, but Shirley never forgot that moment, for in the group of jeering men, she saw her father with a look on his face she had never seen before, and she was frightened, so much so that for days she had to remember the kind loving father she had always known and try to forget… (950)

Quiet Time
by Nick Romeo

I SIT INSIDE PANERA BREAD eating a chicken fruit salad, while my wife takes a class in sewing at a fabric store down the road, and I'd like to say that it's always nice to have soul searching quiet time, so I don't mind driving across town, over at least two bridges, and through three construction zones on a work night just to find out where my soul went, and let me mention how delicious this salad is, fortunately, because it wasn't too expensive — I only had to sell my future first born and left kidney — so I'm glad I had a coupon, and now my ears tune in to a conversation two ladies are having at a table in front of me, the blonde juggling a note pad and pen, while the short-haired brunette uses a laptop as the blonde announces times for the wedding party to arrive, wedding party to take pictures, start of the reception, the toast, the first dance, and who is banned from attending, as the short-haired brunette plugs the data into her computer while voicing her ideas, which agree with the blonde, well, obviously the blonde is the one getting married, and I'm also going to guess that the short-haired brunette is the wedding coordinator, and I'm also going to guess the short-haired brunette is not married, since those who can't do, teach, but I didn't check for a ring, since that's just weird, and besides it next-to-never means anything anyway, because some wear rings as a deflector shield to block advances and others take their rings off in order to receive advances, when the blonde interrupts my thoughts with a mention of a rope-cutting ceremony, and now I am really intrigued, but I hope my spying hasn't become noticeable, because I'd hate to be kicked out for being a creep… could you imagine me trying to explain to my wife why the police came into Panera Bread and dragged me to my car and then tasered me, plus this salad is so tasty, and that's the real reason why I don't want to be kicked out by the Panera Bread's Crack Security Team, and anyway, I wonder if this rope cutting ceremony is a pagan custom, and no, I'm not going to look it up on Whackepedia, because it's not that important to me, but it is interesting how the traditional marriage has been put aside in our culture, most likely because traditional religion has made headlines for mass murder and child abuse, but then pagan religions are also guilty of the same crimes, and they are also traditional religions, because paganism has been around since the dawn of humanity as well, plus or minus a few years, but I bet she didn't think of that one, maybe I'll walk over and tell her — or maybe not — the rope cutting ceremony might simply mean that they will hang the groom from a noose, and she will have to cut him down before he chokes to death, or maybe she'll just decapitate him with the cake cutter, and I'd tell her that if I would ever do it again, get married, that is, I wouldn't have a traditional service either, because first off, I would never get married again, and trust me, this is the first time/last time, and I couldn't imagine going through the dating scene again, but if I did, here's how I would talk while on a date:

    Hello, what is your name?
        (wait for a response)
    What are your hobbies?
        (wait for a response)
    Oh that's really cool. How long have you done that?
        (wait for a response)

even though this non-discussion defies the Geneva Convention just for me to type it out, and if somehow I did feel the need to get married, I would simply buy a Russian, Venezuelan, or African bride over the Internet, since Amazon dot com and Ebay always have sales, but I wouldn't trust Ebay because the items are never as advertised, and if I did get married again, it would be an epic experience, I'm talking fire-breathers, chainsaw jugglers, and obese trapeze artists who don't use nets, and the event would be held inside an explosive factory… but then I'm just kidding… still, I would actually have a sci-fi wedding, and the chapel (no I wouldn't have a chapel) would be decorated like a Star Destroyer, and the civil officiant would be dressed as Boba Fett with a fully functional jet pack and flame thrower, and the reception would be held at a black light cosmic paint ball arena/Sarlacc Pit, where we would separate into teams — the wife and I versus the in-laws — and my second choice would be a Big Stupid Greek wedding, where my bride-to-be would be placed inside a maze, with her mom dressed as a Minotaur, and I would have to find her before the Minotaur does, then I would have to find the civil officiant who would be dressed as Theseus, and he would have to complete the proceedings before the Minotaur arrives, but at least this wedding ceremony wouldn't lag or drag on, and on, and on, and on and on and… for longer than necessary, but then, this wedding being Greek themed would make it a traditional wedding, so disregard this idea, suddenly it sounds like these two ladies at the next table are just about finished with their horribly boring special day plans, because they just used two of the usual phrases we state at so many meetings at work: "I'm glad we're on the same page" and "let's meet again to discuss this further", and anyway it's about time for me to pick up the wife, so I will finish the last few bites of this salad, and complete these last few notes regarding the conversation that I just overheard… (976)

It's Heart Surgery for Goodness Sake
by Barbara Wyatt

I FEEL AWKWARD, UNCOMFORTABLE, unwelcomed, and unable to escape, for after all, I am the caregiver, I am the one my cousin asked to help with his post-heart surgery recovery — it's heart surgery for goodness sake — so I spent $550 of my own money flying 2,665 miles at the last minute to take care of his children and monitor his care, and I knew the first thing I must do was comfort him with reminders that we live in a country with great medical care and his doctor is a highly recommended specialist with six medical staffers to hover over him during the operation, which ended up with me carpooling the kids to and from school, an hour's drive each way, and preparing breakfasts, lunches, and dinners because that's what families must do for each other in times of emergency, and there may be another chore to drive Daniel and his daughter to an evening father/daughter school event planned for one day after his release from the hospital if he is well enough, so, naturally the surgery went smoothly and I picked up Daniel from the hospital on Thursday when more responsibilities were added to my plate to monitor his post-surgery health and blood pressure and do all that is necessary to ensure a successful recovery, yet the very next day he was antsy and wanted to return immediately to a normal routine, which caused Daniel to jump in the passenger seat to drive the one-hour commute to drop off the children at school, even though he was a bit loopy and confused, saying how the doctor told him to "return to your normal activities", but I think he forgot the doctor's full statement was to return to his activities slowly, so after the kids were dropped off, he argued how it would be fun to go shopping at Sam's Club, where we walked for hours until it was time to retrieve the children from school and, of course, he started to fall asleep in the passenger's seat on the drive home until his daughter woke him and said they had to go to that evening's father/daughter event at school that included games on a hard gym floor with no chairs and way too much excitement for someone one day after heart surgery, and I didn't like it because he had been loopy that morning and falling asleep on the drive home, and I was uncertain what to do, but I thought if I waited in the car and he became tired, he could rest or even sleep in the car, so when the daughter slipped on a little blue shift with a tiny flowered pattern, I took a photo and she said, "It's time to go," and I grabbed my laptop and Daniel came down the stairs dressed in khaki pants and a green-collared shirt and announced, "I'm driving," which threw me for a loop because I knew to allow him behind a wheel so soon after heart surgery was a bad idea, so I told him how excited I was to drive them to the event, and I wanted to remind him about his being loopy in the morning and falling asleep in the car, but I understood he was afraid and fragile emotionally and desperately wanted to be normal again, yet the fact it was heart surgery for goodness' sake, and though I understood his emotions, I stayed positive and said, "Let's go," with a big smile and he responded, "No, I am driving, just me and my daughter," and I reminded him that I was happy to go and I had my laptop with its big mega-battery, and he said, "If I can't drive I'm not going," which, needless to say, shocked me, but I must stand strong as a good caregiver, so I repeated that I was looking forward to the drive even though I wasn't because it was a two-hour drive on a rainy night and that's when I reminded him he was loopy in the morning and falling asleep in the car, but I know the event was important to them and I wanted them to be safe, so when he stomped up the stairs and said, "I'm not going," my eyebrows arched in surprise, but I pleasantly said, "I'm headed to the car and ready to go," where I waited and waited and waited and finally the daughter came out and asked, "Can you please let him drive?" and I said I can't because he was loopy that morning and falling asleep in the car and he was released from the hospital a little more than twenty-four hours ago, and I stood ready with my mega-battery laptop to take them to the event, so she returned to the house and I waited and I waited, but no one came out to the car, so I entered the house to find them watching a movie and Daniel said, "The issue is over," and I said, "But I've been waiting to drive you to this father/daughter event that was so important," and he said, "It started at six and now it's too late," and I said, "Then why did you leave me in the car waiting?" and he didn't have an answer because he knew that an adult wouldn't behave that way, and I said the three of us needed to discuss the issue, and he said, "No we don't," and I felt awkward and uncomfortable because I was a guest in the home, but he stayed silent in his tantrum, so I told the daughter that if she was ever loopy and falling asleep one day, I would hold her car keys and drive her wherever she wanted because I loved her, and there was silence while he pretended to watch the movie and ignore me, and I was left feeling awkward and uncomfortable, but my cousin Daniel and his daughter are alive and not mangled in a car wreck on a dark rainy night, to which I conclude that being a caregiver is a thankless job that could mean being trapped 2,665 miles from home. (1033)

Karmic Fishing Trip
by Terry Sager

HE DESERVED IT, HE WAS SUCH A JERK — Jake the Jerk — that's what I secretly called him, but even so, I could deal with him since most people have a little bit of "jerk" in their DNA, and yet he was that guy people never told the truth about, pretending he was this great neighbor, nice guy, would give the shirt off his... oh please, don't even say it because I knew they were all lying, they were afraid of him after all, and this self-delusion included my wife, but I knew the truth because I received many complaint calls about him, most of which I ignored because I've always tried be the bigger man, as they say, and rise above it and all, but he went too far this time, and I refuse to feel guilty since it's his fault anyway, not mine — he's just plain mean, well, was mean — and no one is going to miss him, not me, not anyone, and I knew it was time to take action last evening when I was unloading groceries from the truck — my wife has a bad back, so I help out — and he must have been watching from his front yard because suddenly he appeared from out of the dark (nearly scared me to death) and started talking to me all friendly-like about nonsense, like he always does, and which I totally hate, and he said he was going fishing at sunrise the next morning, and that's when I really started to listen when he said, "Fish bite better in the rain," like I cared (I didn't ask for a weather report), I just wanted to know where he was going fishing, but he just kept on talking about lures and bait and poles, giving me way more information than I wanted to hear, and it made my brain ache, which on top being pissed about what he'd done, I was even more irritated, and then, for the first time since I've known him, he actually did something decent, he asked me if I wanted to go with him, oh yes, yes, I did, but I told him I'd meet him there because Cricket Lake wasn't far and I had some things to do first, but yes, I'd meet him there tomorrow at sunrise and I'd bring coffee (so nice of me), and like the idiot he is, he smiled and said, "Cool, buddy," well, let's get this one thing straight, I am not his buddy, but I need him to think I am, so since he freaking invited me, I didn't have to plan, because even great plans can go terribly wrong, and it was like a sign that all I had to do was show up, when it's the right thing to do, the stars align or something, and everything just goes your way, it's eerie how that happens… and when he finally stopped talking and went back across the yard to his house my phone rang in my ear, I tapped my Bluetooth earpiece to answer it, and No One was there — No One is always there, so it's not like I'm alone in this, No One listens, people hear me, but No One listens — making me think about all this Bluetooth stuff and how you hear people talking on their phone and you just assume there is someone on the other end of the conversation and well, maybe there is, and I think it's a wonderful world where people are so connected, but so disconnected at the same time, so anyway, I get to the lake before sunrise — I hate mornings — so I was already in a bad mood which helped me do what I had to do, and Jake the Jerk was there, waving and walking toward me, and I saw a fish dangling from his line, and wondered when the right moment would come, and as if on cue, Jake said, "Just in time" (how perfect is that), and he handed me that fish bat (yes, there is such a thing) and as he held the poor gasping beast on the ground, he told me to hit it in the head, and put it out of its misery, but I couldn't bear to hurt any animal and so I couldn't give the fish its final blow, well, it just seemed like the perfect time to put Jake out of his misery (or rather my misery), I mean, he did give me the fish bat, so it was kind of like he was asking for it, and that was that, pretty easy, I'd say, and soon I saw the fish still flopping on the ground, so I released it back to the lake and rolled Jake in after it, thinking maybe it could feed on him for a change… so I was thinking how things go so well sometimes, but then I saw that Jake, inconsiderate as always, had splattered me with his blood, not as bad as it could have been since it was raining, which made my cheap rubber pants and parka pretty slick, but even so, I had to clean up a little in the lake, and man, that water was cold, and Jake was sort of bobbing nearby, so after I left "the scene" I dumped the rubber clothes in a Walmart trash can and drove home, and so then I was back in my shop, the rain pounding on the metal roof, soothing me, making me feel so much better, and I get cleaned up in the little bathroom I installed just for times like these, and go into the house, figuring when they find Jake, they'll never connect his demise to me, after all, we were "buds" and I'll be so upset to hear the sad news which I'm sure my wife will tell me since she seems to know everything that happens in the neighborhood, but funny thing is, she doesn't know about me, and she'll keep the horrible news from the children as long as possible so as not to upset them, and we'll have dinner as usual (not fish), and as I'm falling asleep in my warm bed tonight, I will answer Jake's question, the one he asked as I delivered the second and final blow (they always want to know why), but I don't think Jake heard the answer that I told him anyway: "I saw you whack Jangles with a stick because she was napping in your garden, and I guess she went into shock or something because she was dead in the morning, and I know, she's just a cat, but she didn't do you any harm, and she mattered to me — it's all about karma, buddy…" (1125 words)

New Beginnings... Again
by Crystal Perryman

As I embark on a new beginning, I share my amazement of my long journey my siblings and I took to make us the first in the family to be born in the United States, and I still haven't figured out why, but we were, something I learned by going home back to my homeland, Panamá where I had learned to honor my elders, to understand that being quiet was not a weakness but was wise, in that I heard and learned many different languages that opened my eyes and mind to two different worlds, things that I knew other people would never understand, so I try very hard to be patient and humble towards others, not because it is weakness, but because it is a strength knowing that in every story there's a lesson to be learned, and in my homeland I was taught to be me from birth, who I am, where I come from, and the history of my land, and while I understood that being born in another country, my roots remain a blessing, that I could speak dual languages with a native tongue at any given time, a sign of prosperity that makes me to be considered an impressive child in my country, which is why I loved living in Panamá, even though I only have vague memories about home, so when my siblings and I went back in the mid-1980s, to Panamá, the little upside-down S-country holding up the Panama Canal, I discovered I am an indigenous from one of the Seven Wonders of the Modern World, the territory where I recalled being able to have a garden in the backyard of my *abuelita's* house (paternal grandmother) in Pilón, Panamá, where my daddy was raised and where I remember many days just eating our happy souls full to content with *mamones, mangos, marañón curazaos,* for my abuelita had a platter of fruits and vegetables from her garden, and I can still hear her sculling us through the living room window, yelling at the top of her lungs, *"Those pivas aren't ready yet! Leave them alone, children, and you guys are some rude butt children,"* to which all of us children would jump out and scatter through the fields and away from Abuelita, down to the bay to sit on the dock, which was no more than about 300 feet away and was the best place to eat *marañón curazao* (Syzygium malaccense), a fruit that looks like a pear with red skin and white on the inside with a brown seed that looks like an avocado pit, but there were other unforgettable memories, such as the *Carnival*, a water fight parade, where wetsuits are needed, every year in February in the port city of Portobelo, that holds the "Festival de Diablos y Congos", featuring Los Diablos tú tú, young men in the village dressed up in costumes that have extremely large, red and black devil-looking faces, which are really handmade, decorative, sometimes enormous masks that took countrymen days to make, and they carried whips that sometimes matched their masks, and a couple of them wore little tiny bells on their calves so you could hear when they walked toward you, causing Los Congos to conquer and toy with the diablos tú tú, and the other people in the village taunted the Diablos tú tú so that they fled with their devils wielding whips, and then appeared Los Congos, el Rey, a blackface dressed in tattered clothes with a hat representing the crown of victory and carrying a wooden staff as a sword, and all I know is that every February this is our tradition that continues for four or five days straight, with dancing, eating, singing, Polleras, Diablos Espejito, with our ferries and flutes all decorated, and loud speakers everywhere, for Panama is a country widely known for parades and fiestas, such as during the month of November when the flag and patriotic symbols are displayed everywhere for a full month to celebrate Panama separating from Columbia and declaring independence from Spain with countrymen singing this song everywhere, *"Panameño, Panameño, Panameña, vida mía yo quiero que tú me lleves al tambor de la alegría"*, but my time back home was short-lived due to a divorce between my mommy and daddy, one staying in Panamá and the other in the United States, and there were days when I daydreamed about my birth land, the U.S., because Panamá didn't have watermelons or Washington red apples or ice cream trucks or sunny California beaches, Knott's Berry Farm, and Disneyland, so that when my siblings and I came back to the United States in the early 1990s, my second home for me, Panamá, remains where everything started for me, but I had many relatives in New York City, the Big Apple, and I heard stories of the city and listened attentively how my maternal grandmother and how the family got to America after my grandmother's youngest sister, my great-aunt, married a soldier from New York City by way of winning a bet between him and his soldier buddies who challenged my grandfather he could never get a woman as beautiful and refined as my great-aunt, but he won and they married, even though she always complained that New York was too cold to live in, which is why some of my family members journeyed to sunny California in the early-to-mid-1970s, and later, living in Venice Beach, I learned about gangs and drugs and decided to leave, which is when I headed for the Evergreen State of Washington and the City of Destiny, Tacoma, in the mid-'90s, where I soon learned about snow and the first time in my life I saw and touched snow, I loved it, because the snow was stunning and as fast as it came and as fast as it left, I could always see it atop Mount Rainier, and soon became familiar with the Bite of Seattle, the Taste of Tacoma, Henry Foss High School, the Daffodil Parade in Tacoma, and the Super Sonics, the Mariners, and the Seahawks, and the Space Needle in Seattle, and while I woke up every morning in Hawaii for almost a year and witnessed the fiery lava flow of Kilauea, sailing along the Napali Coast, sipping mai-tais in Maui and clubbing in Honolulu, I soon realized that these eyes have seen so many things and will see more, because I just know I am not going to sit here and lie to my children or anyone else for that matter, for if I don't tell you the truth, then surely you will perish and that's why I have to tell you this: there are only a few top rules to follow, and if you can keep those rules, then life will give you more abundance, so follow me, for I would love to take us on this quest for honor and higher education in our community and in yourself by doing the things in daily etiquette that will honor The Divine Providence with all our hearts and minds, because by honoring yourself and your neighbor, by honoring your parents, your children, their children, and their children's children will honor us forever, and one other thing, please forgive your parents and others and, above all, forgive yourself. Keep love holy! (1221)

Distractions in a Suitcase
by Judy Ashley

It's been a few years now since Mom passed on and, after the heirs took their fond remembrance items, four estate sales, and numerous garage sales, all that is left to sort through are a couple of suitcases overstuffed with photographs, one box, and a large trunk of memorabilia that is one of those overwhelming projects I tend to procrastinate doing while telling myself there is always tomorrow and meanwhile allowing the room where they are stored to become the catch-all room until one day my stress level reaches the top and I can stand it no longer so I begin to sort, straighten, categorize, remember, feel sad, become depressed, and realize this task is entirely too overwhelming so I immediately retreat to another room where I grab a snack and play a video game which helps me to focus and calms my frustrations and I do not feel guilty because at least I started the project and will invariably get back to it tomorrow or the next day, and meanwhile my brain is tweaking the ingenious plan I devised to break down this mind-boggling sorting task into smaller manageable ones which is necessary due to the enormous quantity of photos piled up in duplicates, triplicates, and often quadruplicates because way back then, before cameras on cellphones, my uncle would take pictures (lots and lots of pictures), develop them in at least triplicate and give one of each to my mom, my aunt, and sometimes to me and, of course, when my uncle passed on, my mom inherited his photos duplicating her own set plus some she didn't have and then, when my aunt passed, Mom inherited a third set of the same photos and, although they were in a few neatly put-together albums, the majority of the pictures were loosely bound in their little print envelopes along with the negatives (in case we needed more copies of the copies we already had) and I, in my astute wisdom, immediately discarded all envelopes, landscape photos not of display quality, along with all the negatives thereby greatly reducing the total quantity to sort and, oh, I think I forgot to mention the 35-mm slides that also need to be sorted and appropriately distributed or discarded, and I am attempting to sort these items but find the task dreadfully time consuming as I become frightfully distracted every time I come upon something that I have never seen before or something particularly interesting like some photographs that my father had hid away in a small metal box in the back of a closet and which now sits in the front of my closet waiting, beckoning me to decipher the true meaning of it all, so I sit back and look closely at the pictures of my dad from World War II — my dad with people I don't know, my dad in Europe, so good looking, so young — so much I wanted to know but there is no one left to ask and then I come across a three-ring binder containing Dad's smartly organized work history, his Army Air Corps days during World War II, and as I read these papers for the first time, answers to questions that I had wanted to ask years ago now reveal themselves along with explanations about other things I'd often wondered about and which now seem to make sense although there are still many unanswered questions, and while Dad did share with me some events from his mysterious war days, he never completely divulged his memories, or perhaps he did not even remember certain events himself, or maybe he didn't want to remember them, but he did seem to enjoy some fond memories of his time in England during the war and I don't mind telling you that he was something special — good looking, strong slender physique with broad shoulders, smart, quick-witted and a bit mysterious at times — and, of course, there were many things he never talked about but here I go again, rambling on and on about my dad when I am supposed to be working on this sorting task, but I suspect that you can now empathize with my dilemma and see how distractions can delay completion of this project and how easily I can completely lose track of time and forget what it is I was supposed to be doing and, in case you haven't guessed, my dad is no longer residing with the living since he passed on ten years before my mom and it's true that he and I were very close and many people think I'm very much like him, for which I'm glad, but again I digress, and there is so much more to learn and decipher as I pull out diaries belonging to my great-grandfather on my mother's side who was a preacher in England who never saw the United States (his son, my grandfather, immigrated to the U.S. via Ellis Island) and look at this, a whole book of his sermons beautifully handwritten in Olde English that might as well be a foreign language and yes, I do believe I have discovered another project — translating these papers — so I'll set these aside for another day and move on to our next find in this trunk full of ancestral revelations and oh, there's Mom's lists and all her daily happenings marked on those little purse calendars, many years' worth, all neatly bundled with rubber bands and yes, it's true that if you wanted to know what Mom was doing on a particular day at a specific time seven years ago, I'm sure I could find the answer in this pile of calendars but, moving on, I now find myself reading my grandmother's diaries containing pages and pages of ordinary everyday occurrences like making bread, going to the market, "Li'l Ruthie (my mom) was sick today" or so-and-so came to visit today, but no expression of feelings so I can only guess what she was thinking, but now I am too emotionally exhausted to think straight after reviewing these items and am realizing how little I truly know of my relatives' lives before my time and I'm feeling a bit guilty for not caring when there were still people alive who could answer my questions and tell me things that I wanted to know and, oh sure, I could do historical research, theorize, and then, together with what I do know and what I have been told through the years, I could draw some fairly accurate conclusions, but that leaves too much room for error and filling in the blanks leaves too much to the imagination, but perhaps it doesn't really matter or perhaps it's not as romantic as I want to believe or maybe there really are deep secrets hidden away in that suitcase or, perchance, there was someone long ago in a different time who looked and acted just like me and yes, the possibilities are endless or, more likely, it's only my imagination running wild or wishful thinking and maybe all of this will prove to be merely ordinary and mundane and I shall probably not come to any specific conclusions, but will return to this pile of pictures, letters, and documents from another era and simply enjoy my sorting project, and I shall smile while remembering, imagining, and encountering delightful distractions as I glimpse into the lives of people who lived in a different world in a different time and who share my DNA and, perhaps, one day I may even finish this project. (1259)

Escape the Dark
by Terry Sager

JOE USES THE LOBBY INTERCOM to let our host know we are on our way up and to make sure a chair is ready for me, because this time I am going to tell the truth the first chance I get, and after riding up seventeen floors in silence we arrive, and almost as soon as he rings the doorbell our host opens the door and enthusiastically ushers us in, but I barely have a chance to say hello before Joe lays on the charm as usual, and by the end of the party even the men will be taken in by him, or should I say "fooled" by him, and almost as if I'm an afterthought, the host finally notices me again and guides me to large comfy chair, and as I sit, she fusses over me a few seconds asking how I'm doing, and I want to tell her, but I can't right now since Joe is still nearby, close enough I can smell him, and as someone places a stemless glass in my hand, the bouquet of a pinot is intoxicating as Joe pats my arm (I cringe) and tells me he's going to mingle… and I too am acquainted with most of the guests, fewer and fewer as the years go by, and as my sight has retreated, I recognize them mostly by voice or scent, and sometimes by their shoes, and some will stop by my chair, utter the obligatory hello and get back to the party, and I fear my blindness makes them nervous, but they don't know it scares the hell out of me, and it has caused me to be a prisoner of someone I don't know, or rather barely know, because I was married to Joe's father for only six months, one of my most grievous mistakes, but I never thought of Joe as a son because he was away most of the time, so I never really knew him at all… then suddenly, Alice's cackle jerks me out of my reverie, like thunder rolling across an open prairie, the sound startling everyone in its path (I think she's gotten louder over the years, or perhaps her volume was easier to handle when I was sighted), but now my other senses are much sharper, more sensitive, and I begin to wonder if could tell Alice, and maybe she'll stop by my chair later, yes, I'll tell her then, but in the meantime I think about the many years I have been invited to these networking things and I am beginning to tire of them, but Joe wants to be here and everybody loves Joe because they think of him as my devoted son who escorts me, his aging, blind mother, to her much-loved events, and no one knows the truth of it, that it's a command performance orchestrated by Joe, and I am only his ticket through the door, and oh yes, I realize he's a user, and I need to be rid of him, and fortunately, I'm not totally blind — I can still see around the edges of my vision — but Joe thinks I am, and I need that small bit of advantage, and as I take a sip of the chilled pinot and press the cool glass to my cheek, giving me momentary relief from the noisy, stifling room that is filling with the regular mentors, and there are the hopeful newbies (I don't recognize their voices), who are the younger people trying to make the connection that will change their future, and while I used to enjoy them and my advice was sought after, but no longer, few talk to me — maybe Joe has told them I prefer to be left alone because that way no one will get close enough for me to tell — I sit back, glad that at least this time my chair is comfortable and a bit out of the main flow of people, and I begin to enjoy my invisibility until a bejeweled stiletto trips over my foot, says nothing in the way of apology, but only chirps about how embarrassing it would have been if she fell — I personally would have rather enjoyed that — perhaps my feet, in their fashionable (yet orthopedic) slippers appeared in her path on purpose, just saying maybe, I have to get my kicks somehow, then I recognize Marco as he sashays in my direction, hearing the jangling of his gaudy jewelry getting louder as he gets closer, and I smell Old Spice and wonder if it is still *en vogue*, or maybe it's his hair gel I smell, either way, I've known him since the '70s and the only thing that has changed is that he is no longer that hip young designer wearing too much of everything, including gold chains, he's just an aging queen, but no matter, he knows it and is perfectly happy, so maybe I could tell Marco, but he only pats me on the hand and tells me how lovely I look and continues on his way, and the voices in the room drone on like a meditation, soothing until a Helen or a Bob speaks or laughs just a little too loud, shattering the peace, but all in all, lulled by the wine, it's rather pleasant to sit and absorb the sounds and scents of humanity, but then there is a rather harsh tap on my shoulder and I am fully back to my present reality, a present that has become a prison, and despite the stuffy room, a shiver runs through me as Joe has come to fetch me, it's time to go, and as he helps me to my feet, his grip too tight, he arranges my hand on his forearm and guides me to the door telling me, as if we are great friends, he's met some very interesting people, to which I just smile and nod (like I care), and once again we are in the lobby and as he opens the door, the cool night air refreshes me as we walk the one block to the subway, and I know I have missed my chance again, but who can I really trust anymore, who would believe he makes me accompany him to parties and made me give him the PIN to my bank account, or maybe he's told them it's not just my eyesight that is failing me, but also my mental faculties, being old and blind isn't as bad as it sounds, it's just been bad since Joe showed up, and I must escape the dark he has visited upon me, and so every night before I fall asleep, I try to think of how I could rid myself of this thirty-something crook, because even if I got caught and went to prison, it would be better than the prison I am in now, and as we wait on the platform, I drop my purse, oh silly me, and as Joe squats to pick it up, his back to me, my rascal of a stylish orthopedic slipper connects perfectly to his lower back and he tumbles onto the tracks, oh, how lovely, the train is on time, and in the ensuing chaos, I retrieve my purse, luckily he didn't have a grip on it when he fell, and I, oh so theatrically, bring my hands to my face, the horror of it all, and now people are screaming and yelling and I know that once the police arrive they will arrange a ride home for me for, after all, they will take pity on the old woman whose attendant has just died horribly, *no officer, I'm nearly blind, I didn't see what happened*, pity I will have to contain my glee until I get home safe and sound, still old, still almost blind, but finally alone again, finally free again…(1316)

The Drugstore on the Corner
by Val Dumond

THIS WAS ONE OF THOSE DAYS when Junie was feeling so special about herself she wanted to eat cake with her morning coffee, but not at home, at the corner drugstore down the street, where she had worked for so many years but now was "retired", as they say on Wall Street, but she didn't feel like sitting around or knitting baby blankets for the homeless, so she took herself off to the corner drugstore down the street after sleeping late for a change, just to have herself a special kind of breakfast at the popular and often busy lunch counter, which she knew wouldn't be too crowded on a lovely day like this, except for maybe a couple of workmen or maybe an early shopper or two, the kind of folks who eat breakfast at the corner drugstore, but she wasn't expecting the fun she was going to have as she walked through the door and saw a couple of old workmates busily sprucing up the store for the day's business, like Maizy, the tall lean woman over there wearing an apron as she goes about with her dust cloth, tidying up the shelves and displays, or Janice, that always chatty friendly waitress over there behind the lunch counter, pouring coffee for the work crew from City Hall who frequent the place for their breaks, or someone like Rose, who always has a smile on her rosy cheeks and good words for everyone she meets, even the cranks who sometimes are nuts enough to complain about something that a natural human person would never think of complaining about, and over there in front of the grill stands Wanda, that pretty little creature who can cook up in just a couple of minutes a fried egg sandwich you wouldn't believe, a sandwich you'd remember all day long because she makes it with a handful of chives and a dollop of sour cream, delicately mixed and fried all together with the best sourdough bread you've ever tasted, but that wasn't what Junie came for that day because it was so special, that day that she decided to have a lovely piece of Wanda's melt-in-your-mouth chocolate cake with double-fudge frosting for breakfast, along with a cup or two of the wonderfully aromatic coffee that the best drugstores pour for their customers, and she expected to sit back, savor the moment, josh a bit with her friends, and make it a day that she'd always remember, that special day… but that was about to be quashed by a bunch of little girls, the kind Junie used to be when she grew up in this great little town on the Koshkonong River, so many, many… well maybe not *that* many years ago… because little girls on summer vacation behave like little girls on summer vacation, dressing up in their best pair of shorts and tee shirts, combing out the curls they set with old socks in their hair the night before after sneaking into Mom's room to "borrow" a tinge of lipstick, just enough to brighten up their faces, but not enough for Mom to notice and make her remove, and when Junie walked into the drugstore, there they were, over in the corner at the magazine counter, a passel of them giggling as they huddled around the latest copy of *Esquire* with its glossy photos of young women strung all the way through the pages, little girls knowing that one day they would look like that — maybe if they paid attention to brushing their hair and drinking the milk that produced lovely finger- and toe-nails — and not even looking up as the store manager, Mr. Bruce, approached, stood over them, and uttered an "Ahem" that startled them as well as scattered them momentarily, which caused Junie to smile a bit, remembering her own moments as she walked up to the counter to place her breakfast order, which she managed to do rather quickly since Janice was ever alert to new customers as she quickly placed a cup on the counter and poured the blissfully aromatic first cup of the day for Junie, who smiled knowingly as she told Jan about her special day and special decision for her breakfast meal, which was reacted to with one of Janice's best smiles and a song that sounded like "This Is Your Day" but came out more like "Homer Jones' Bones" because her sweet trilling good-morning voice couldn't carry a tune if she put it in a pail, but Jan had tried and that made Junie even happier as she carried the cup over to the booths to await her chocolate cake with double-fudge frosting, hopeful as she was, however she came to a stop to peruse the situation that she found ahead of her, that was not the blissful day she had planned but a rather peculiar obstacle she must overcome before she could enjoy herself, because what she saw when she approached the booth section of the corner drugstore was a few of those little girls occupying each of the booths provided by the luncheonette section for its customers, one little girl on each side of each table, poring over the menu, looking for something cheap to buy to accompany her soda, as the store had a policy of insisting on customers buying food when they occupied the booths, and the little girls were raptly occupying the booths as they sought to enjoy their first days of summer with daring actions that could set the course for the entire summer, which Junie could understand because she had "been there, done that" herself, and that was when Maizy walked by with her handy dust cloth in hand, sauntering up to each booth and one by one dusting the dividers and the legs of the tables and even the tables themselves with her trusty dusty cloth, action that didn't perturb the girls at all, even as Maizy looked at Junie and shrugged her shoulders, but that was when Junie decided there was a better way to clear the booths of the interlopers, to send them to a single booth, the counters, or maybe even out of the store, for Mr. Bruce was not keen on them as customers since they usually messed up those expensive *Esquire* magazines with their grubby fingers and they rimmed his soda glasses with their mothers' lipstick, with a plan that Junie put into action as she casually walked up to the booth in the back corner and plunked herself down, along with the coffee cup, and asked the girls, "Isn't this a lovely day to enjoy a cuppa at the corner drugstore?" which met with blank stares of disbelief from the two girls, one of whom was scrunched up between the wall and Junie's fulsome body, but which brought no remarks from the girls who looked back and forth from each other and to Junie and back again, suddenly drawing attention from the other girls in the other booths who craned their little necks around the sides to see what was going on in the back booth, hearing Junie's voice as she began to regale the girls about "when I was young…" stories of her misbegotten youth at the very same corner drugstore all those years ago, until with one gigantic motion, as if a whistle had been blown or a siren sounded, the girls, every single one of them — except the poor thing who was caught between Junie and the wall — jumped up, tugged at their tee shirts and shook their curls with a show of disgust and began slowly to walk out of the corner drugstore, causing the little scrunched-up girl to call out in desperation, then slowly slide under the booth table, only once catching her hair on the bubble gum stuck there as she crawled out from the booth, mussing her otherwise cutesy self, and she ran to catch up with her friends, a moment that mercifully coincided with the crew from the drugstore on the corner to march up to Junie who sat smiling at herself in the booth raising her arms in victory and then stretching them out to receive the royal plate of chocolate cake with double-fudge frosting, a victorious moment that caused the crew — Maizy, Janice, Wanda, Rose, and even Mr. Bruce — to belt out a chorus of "Happy Birthday, dear Junie" as she settled back in the booth, raised her fork to direct the choir, then bring it down, plunging it into the lovely chocolate cake with double-fudge frosting and taking her first bite of her new birth year, joining in the last chorus with "Happy Birthday to me!" (1448)

Fateful Flight Suit
by Ruth Anderson

Bachelor Officers' Quarters (BOQ) 2013,
Grayson Air Force Base, April 3, 1969

HEAD HOUSEKEEPER DOTTY COLES WAITED impatiently on the sidewalk in front of the large brick officers' quarters on a lovely spring day, impatient because standing outside wasn't getting the work done inside, but Captain Gina Bolt, a base personnel officer, had called her with a cryptic request to meet her outside, so Dotty managed a smile when Bolt drove up and helped a beautiful, young, obviously pregnant woman of Asian descent, the young woman's eyes tired but hopeful, climb out of the car with much bowing and smiling, and Bolt introduced her as Talia Potts who came from a town near Udorn Air Force Base, Thailand, a base Dotty knew from letters she had received from pilots who had trained at Grayson, and both women listened while Talia, speaking very clipped English, told them that her father, a British soldier, stayed in Asia after World War II and was traveling in Thailand where he met and married her mother and opened a restaurant, which was where, last year, Talia had met an American pilot by the name of Greg Blekins, at whose name Dotty and Captain Bolt both gasped, for Captain Greg Blekins, who had lived in Room 218 in the BOQ, had been killed in a training accident near Grayson in January 1968, and it seemed unlikely that someone with the same oddish name would have been a pilot at Udorn, that Talia attempted to explain by producing a photo of a smiling, handsome young man wearing a flight suit with Blekins' name, which further astonished the women, for the person masquerading as Blekins was, in fact,

Airman First Class Bryan Sutterfield, formerly a personnel technician in Captain Bolt's office, and it was he and Bolt who had come to Blekins' BOQ room after the accident to oversee the packing of Blekins' effects, which were sent to the family, and Dotty recalled the day clearly for she had washed all of Blekins' dirty clothes and was folding them on his bed when the team arrived, and somehow, she suggested, Sutterfield must have managed to liberate one of Blekins' flight suits, secure it probably at the bottom of his duffel bag, from whence he retrieved it when he arrived at Udorn for his year of duty, but poor Talia couldn't take in the flow of words as Captain Bolt and Dotty discussed the wherefores, and seeing her near collapse, Dotty put her arm around the young woman and led her into the lobby, while Bolt retrieved the girl's suitcase, Dotty having offered to take the girl home, there being room since her daughter had left for college, and Bolt promised to find out where Sutterfield was since Talia tearfully revealed that they had dated for ten months and then he had apparently left abruptly because she could find no one on base who had ever heard his name, and she thought maybe he had been a pilot on some secret mission that nobody was supposed to know about, and when she discovered she was pregnant, she decided to come to America and look for him because she loved him and he had told her he loved her and wasn't married, but the only location he had ever mentioned was Grayson Air Force Base, so she had obtained a passport and was here to locate her pilot, and Dotty suggested that Lt. Colonel Denforth in the legal office might be of some use, which Bolt noted before departing, leaving Dotty to find an empty room where the girl could get some rest while Dotty finished her work, and so began an interesting search for the culprit who had impregnated a young, trusting woman while impersonating an officer, which brought Lt. Colonel Denforth three days later to the BOQ to question Talia gently, made easier for the rest and care she was receiving from Dotty, and Talia explained that her parents had been pleased when she began dating Greg because he had excellent manners and treated them all very nicely, which was why it all came as such a shock when he suddenly disappeared, and she had begged her father to provide money for her to fly to America and now she was here, pregnant with Greg's baby, and where was he because they had to find him soon because the baby was due in three months, and Lt. Colonel Denforth reported that a retired Air Force Special Investigator had promised to help them find Sutterfield, and a week later Denforth and Bolt brought the investigator, Adam Turbin, to the BOQ to meet with Talia, who insisted Dotty sit in, everyone then learning that Sutterfield had completed five years of duty and been honorably discharged and returned to his home town, Tucson, Arizona, where he had secured a good job with the city's personnel office, and was living alone in a nice-looking apartment building, but his masquerade had not ended, for Turbin had discovered that Sutterfield frequented the Veterans of Foreign Wars (VFW) hall, where he had at least once turned up in a flight suit with the captains' bars and pilot wings still affixed but the nametag missing, which had raised eyebrows but no real concern, and everyone at the club knew him as Captain Sutterfield, nicknamed "Sutty", as he had been known at Grayson, prompting Denforth to note that impersonating an officer was an offense under the Uniform Code of Military Justice, and that he could have faced punishment had it become known while he was on active duty, but now that he had been discharged, perhaps he could be advised that legal proceedings to amend his honorable discharge would be taken unless he lived up to his obligations to Talia, who promptly burst into tears, declaring that she didn't want him to have to marry her but just to meet with her to see the situation she was in, a proposal they all acknowledged would be best, and Turbin promised to accompany Talia to Tucson to meet Sutterfield, and that evening Dotty and Talia went home to plan what she would say when she met the man she would have to learn to call "Bryan", which eventuality commenced six days later when Turbin came to collect her and her suitcase for the flight, it having been decided by all that if Sutterfield wouldn't cooperate, Talia would return to Grayson, where she would live with Dotty until the baby came, but Dotty was not to have the opportunity to host that baby due to Cupid's, and Adam Turbin's, intervention, which Turbin orchestrated by meeting Sutty at his apartment first to cast a look around to see how he was living, most satisfactorily, so mincing no words, Turbin described Talia's dilemma and didn't need to ask if Sutty was the man, because upon hearing Talia's name, Sutty buried his head in his hands before turning to Turbin to say how sorry he was that he had brought that darn flight suit to Thailand and played that game with such a wonderful girl from a good family, and he loved her but just couldn't figure out how to tell her he wasn't what she thought, and the next evening, Turbin took Talia to the apartment and stood by as the two young lovers came together in a ferocious hug that Turbin thought might harm the baby, but before he departed the touching scene, Sutty handed him a large, brown paper bag that held the flight suit, which Turbin returned to Dotty who washed it and had the nametag replaced before sending it on to Blekins' family, whose young son responded by letting her know they were all okay, and he was very happy to get the suit because his older brother got the only other one that was sent to them, and three months later Dotty received photos of a smiling couple with their sweet little girl baby, a dark haired cutie named Manee Dot, who, but for the Vietnam War, would not have been born, and Dotty invited Captain Bolt, Lt. Colonel Denforth, and Adam Turbin to the BOQ, where Turbin produced a small bottle of champagne, so all could toast the happy ending of an impersonation that Denforth assured all present concluded better than most, it being best in life to be honest about your achievements, to which all raised their glasses and then to the real Captain Blekins, whose young life was cut short, and Dotty sat down that evening and wrote another letter to his family, enclosing one of the photos "with the hope that it might assuage your grief to know that Greg's flight suit helped win the heart of a now lovely young mother," which is precisely what Mrs. Blekins thought when she saw the photo and tearfully blessed the little family and the memory of her darling eldest son. (1474)

My New Computer Toy
by Billie A. Stewart

I HAVE A NEW TOY FOR MY COMPUTER and may actually like it someday if I can ever figure out how to use it properly, but I'm not too sure about that, and honestly, it isn't even that new since I bought it a year ago but didn't start using it until this past week because it really intimidated me and I was unsure if it would work right, so I left it in the original box and bag from the store, slowly forgetting that I had it until I talked with my friend, Chris, who said she had the toy too and said she really liked hers and used it all the time, finding it very useful as it saved her time, but I was still pretty skeptical until Chris came over one day to help me install it, and after several unsuccessful attempts, I said, "Bag it," because I was frustrated and decided to leave it alone for a while, waiting weeks to try to install it again (hard to remember exactly how long as time seems to go by so quickly gobbling up everything in its path) but I regress, so I tried installing it again, but it continued giving me error messages, so I looked at the package it came in and saw that only one installation is allowed due to copyright issues, and I thought, wow, I screwed up something because it still wouldn't install as I typed in the serial number, but I'm sure my several attempts using the serial number caused the repeated error messages when I tried installing it because, heaven knows, I'm not a computer techie, yet I can generally hold my own on the computer, but since I'm far from an expert, and if I forget to look at some dumb little detail like how many times one can install some new program, I know I will pay for it in the end with headaches, so I may have to stop for a few minutes and take a couple of aspirins or Tylenol or Aleve (I never remember which is supposed to work best so I will try two aspirins), and stay on task because I don't like interruptions that send me off onto rabbit trails when I'm trying to get something important done, (at least I think installing this new toy is important) and I ask myself why should it matter to anyone else anyway because it's my program, my problem, and my headache if I can't install it correctly after so many tries, and another try or two or three shouldn't matter because the program obviously doesn't like me as much as I think I like it, so I thought the best thing to do was to go back to the store where I bought it nearly a year ago and buy another one and try installing it instead, but I was pretty sure I couldn't take it back since it was way past the purchase date and they wouldn't take it back or give me back my money, so I bought a new one with my credit card and kicked myself because with tax it came to $110, so I brought it home and tried installing it, but danged if I didn't get the same error message as I got on the first one which really ticked me off as I didn't need to add $110 to my credit card for a purchase that didn't work and obviously was trying it's darnedest to frustrate me, but I'm a fighter and was determined not to let some silly computer program win this battle, so I was unwavering in my attempt to continue fighting to the end if necessary (but I didn't know where the end was) and didn't want to tell people that a computer program beat me again, nor did I even mention the other times I got into fights with the computer, and I don't have the time nor the inclination to do so now, but I guess everyone fights with their computers at times, especially my sister, and her computer wins most of the battles, so I was determined to keep fighting until I won and tried installing the new program until the stupid new program gave me the same error message I got from the old program, which led me back to the box it came in where I saw it had website information and a 1-800 number for technical support, so I called and got a man with a very heavy accent (he is probably in India or Pakistan) and he asked me repeatedly to describe my problem, which I did several times until finally he seemed to have a grasp of what I was encountering and at last seemed to understand somewhat, but Techie began chastising me for trying to install both of the programs more than once and referred me to the box the program came in to see where it said only one installation per disk was allowed, and I did the only thing I thought I could under the circumstances by dutifully apologizing for not seeing the message earlier, which seemed to make him happy, and with that he said he would try to help me as he reminded me that both programs had different serial numbers and I shouldn't be getting the error message on the second program that I got on the first one (duh!) and I agreed, but said I got it anyway and all I wanted him to do was to help me get this expensive program loaded onto my computer so I could use it and told him I was frustrated with it because it gave me a headache and I needed to take something for it, (but I didn't tell him that I was going to wait until I saw the ad on television again as I didn't think it was any of his business) so I just let it go as it was sure to confuse him and I certainly didn't want to listen to a confused, heavy-accented techie explain something to me about the program, so I didn't tell him and was glad I didn't because then Techie asked for my email address and other identifying information, which I gave him, and he said he would email the program to me so I could download it and install it with his help and it would take about forty minutes to download and I could call back later if I had any problem, but since I was fixing dinner at the time and had several other things to do and was frustrated enough for one day, I decided to just put the whole thing aside and try it again in the morning, so the following morning when I was fresh and not as frustrated with the whole thing, I checked my email and tried to download what Techie sent me, and once again I got the same error message that I got every time before on both programs (both the older one and the new one) so I called tech support once more and got someone else with a very heavy accent and started the process all over again, and thought, *wow, what fun all of this is*, and I decided that those on-line companies must purposely try to frustrate the rest of us by hiring guys with heavy accents that we can hardly understand and who, in turn, can hardly understand us, just to keep aggravated customers from calling back, but I wasn't quite ready to quit (although I think I was getting closer this time) so after going through all the same scenario again with the new guy, he said he would email it to me and when it down-loaded to my computer, it should install with no problem, and I laughed as I thought, *do I believe this techie dude*? but of course not, but I didn't tell him that, and instead told him to go ahead and email it to me again and I said the other techie-dude emailed it to me yesterday and when I tried to download and install it, I got the same error message that I got all along, but he didn't seem to care that I felt like I was on a merry-go-round and couldn't get off, repeating that it would take forty minutes to down-load, which I'd already heard before, so I just grunted and accepted it and hoped it might actually work this time, so I waited awhile before checking my email and sure enough, Techie II had sent the program again, yet I was very skeptical as I opened it and tried to install it on my computer, and wow, was I ever surprised as it down-loaded and installed as smoothly as possible, which I could hardly believe since the down-loaded version was for the first program that I bought nearly a year ago, so then I decided to try to return the newer one to the store and get my $110 back on my credit card as I could surely use the money for something else, so when I got to the store, I told them something was wrong with the program since I tried to install it and kept getting an "error message" and I had just bought it the day before (but I didn't tell them I tried to install it several times and probably screwed something up inside it), instead, I said it was undoubtedly faulty and the clerk believed me and took the charge off my credit card and I'm sure they will send it back to the company where the techies with the heavy accents will probably fix it in no time and sell it again to someone else who likes new toys, and in the meantime, I have my new toy installed and hope it will finally work properly, but first I'll have to play with it for a while so it gets used to me and me to it, but wait, I didn't tell you about my new computer toy, it's called "Dragon Naturally Speaking" and when we become much better friends than we are now (which I certainly hope will happen) I'm expecting it to help me with my writing as I just need to speak aloud what I want it to write, and it is supposed to just type away, but it makes a lot of mistakes and tells me often that it can't hear me very well because of background noise (which consists of the refrigerator humming and the computer keys clicking) but so far, it is making lots of errors including spelling and grammar mistakes, and it writes things I didn't even say and it continues to frustrate me because I don't think it likes my accent and my way of speaking because it is not used to English or to Americans speaking it anyway, but stay tuned and I'll let you know if things improve as I use it, and I'll keep remembering that my friend, Chris, really likes hers and perhaps one of these days I can say that I really like mine too, but meanwhile, I don't have to watch those television ads for headache pills since I didn't need to take any after all because I won the battle with the computer (this time anyway). (1903)

Pulling on a Thread
by Mr. Miller

THE WALK UPHILL FROM THE TOWN near the beach to the road on the ridge runs a good quarter mile, seems longer and colder in the winter rain, the remains of leaves turning flat and dark where they cover small streams of water along the side of the road, endless steps on black tar and gravel, the greeting this town offers those who turn from the highway above toward the town below, the uncertain sound tires make as they approach the bottom of the hill, a town with no budget for proper asphalt, no welcome for new arrivals, dangerous strangers like the couple three houses down having lived here for years, who still can't be truly trusted, the way it is with winter on Puget Sound, a flash, a streak of sunlight followed by darker clouds, the rain, the wind and waves pushing in toward the beach, the way it was today, half way up the hill with no refuge from the weather, a wet coat, and the chill of the wind, a thin black coat with a hood that made it possible to keep on to avoid a hypothermic shiver, a cold, violent shake as if there was no coat, this place where ancient maples sleep covered in a blanket of moss, a place where tossed cigarette butts come to a lifeless stop, where toxic filtered waste dissolves in the stream that flows and moves over blades of grass in the ditch, a chemical soup draining out into the bay, scattered trash like the kind I sweep and pick up along the front of the house each week because the city has no sweeper, no money to hire it properly done, this work now unworthy of individuals who need the exercise in a way they refuse to understand, the town asking instead in a meek tone for assistance this time of year, to keep a look-out on the drains at the side of the road, keep the ditch clear of leaves, do our part as we all do to hold the place together, the waves creeping higher with the tides each year, the scream of the wind when the gusts shake the trees and anything else not securely tied and locked down, the walking easier near the top of the hill where the bus will stop, the highway they once called 99, as if changing a name changes anything, the way a woman or a man remains essentially unchanged after the vows, the ring, the cake, the rituals, the way an ancient spirit follows along a native path to the beach that becomes a wagon rut and then a wider, modern Model-T road, all that did nothing to change the slope of the hill, this waterfront spit with a line of homes where the longhouse stood before it was burned, a collection of stubborn people who see no need for a bus, no reason to lower carbon emissions, offset the wood smoke of winter fires that mix with the coal plant's electric breath blowing out of the southwest this time of year, the gun-like crack of Arctic ice sheets muffled by the vehicles on old historic 99, four lanes full they shuffle past, a spray of road rain spinning off of the tires, dripping from under every vehicle, until finally a bus appears in the distance, the lights near the top form into numbers, the words "Federal Way" promise somewhere to sit, a warm space, clanky mechanical rumblings the earphones ignore, pushed away to a comfortable distance, everyone seeking a personal space, a seat on the bus, a place near the fire, at a concert, opera, or ballet, sharing the experience in a collective sense, equals in a democratic spatial plane, expecting the occasional injustice, hunger and pain, socks a week between washing, a story of lives explained by plastic bags with their bulging contents, a hat, a warm, worn coat, bandaged arms, coughs, lost consciousness, a head nodding down, sleeping with a dream as the tavern slips by and the bus rounds the corner almost up to speed, approaching a small town in the distance where the world of make believe hides everything in a mist, the smoke shops, a casino, a wide empty sidewalk, the vacant lot where a motel once stood, where the kid who pitched with his left hand lived, the three-story house on the opposite side of the highway, gone with farm after farm, barn by barn becoming pieces of scrap paved over with asphalt lanes between warehouse blocks, their mushrooming cold concrete walls like the soil, never again to see the light of day, the bus approaching the bridge above the river then on down desolate avenues where everyone digs into their pockets to find a fare, those who encounter misfortune or luck, all of us there together on a bus riding on toward destiny, school, work, to the end of the line on Commerce Street where commercial activity was long ago condemned and evicted, a mean vision of urban renewal that favored lots for parking, the bus stops in alphabetical order, real estate investments, the litter and dirt in the gutter that are noticeable as the rear bus door opens, the cold air blasts against your face, where a path must be negotiated with a careful step around the garbage can lying on its side, motionless, dead to the world, where someone dug through the trash for a scrap of food, searched for somewhere to sleep far enough away from the sound of the lonely peep at the stop light, the digital words shouting "Wait" at the courthouse crossing, the metallic, robotic announcements on the bus, suddenly, all gone silent, this street where time in its way slows and almost stops when waiting on a bus, where hope seems lost, then a few scattered rays of sun slip between buildings to share a secret slowly silenced, drowning in fog that settles and washes away the evidence of life from every shadow, quiets every voice, the cold wind between and around the people on the street, that makes footsteps hurry and rush away up the hill past a theater marquee, the daycare for dogs, away from everything that can't be rescued, healed, or repaired, makes a person desperate to reach the bookstore, watching the sign in the distance, a block more, just beyond the medical facility, the shuttle parked outside where eyes turn away, reflexive, wanting not to see the man up ahead moving at a slow, careful pace, an older, tired, pale face, a wisp of hair and a worn wool jacket, no hat or gloves, small measured steps suggesting some invisible, internal issue, left hand gripping his chrome metal cane with its four tiny feet, he smiling as I pass, his teeth stained and imperfect, polished wire rim glasses firmly in place, and he asks how I am, I who have everything he does not, fortunate enough to ride a bus and walk up a hill in the rain, he asks with a soft voice how I am and without a thought I respond, I am well, about to pick up a book that will change my life, as all other books have not yet done, that part of the explanation I do not share, instead I hurry on, unsettled by his words, in an urgent rush, not thinking to stop and ask the same of him because there is no room in my head or my heart, no space for one burden more, but looking back, it would have been such a small thing to invite him to the pub for a pint and there, as the drinks were delivered, a secret we would keep from the caregiver, a blink of two pairs of eyes, almost in unison, if I had asked he might have told me his story, that unique tale everyone knows by heart and there for a time we would sit, I would listen, and together later we would pick up the book, find one for him, walk back to his residence, his way-station, a metaphorical bus stop of life, watching his step perhaps improved by the pint, maybe not, but I will never know these things because in a rush, a hungry need to hold a book that might reveal the secret of life, I told the man simply that I was well, smiling back in a confused sort of way as I turned and hurried on to the bookstore, then back downtown, back to the bus and opened to a page in the third chapter about the muse, the care and feeding of feral spirits, invisible as a naked night breeze, skittish, a sometimes impossible distance as remote and removed as the human side of an animal enclosure at the zoo, the way reflections are mirror-like, the real in an unreal form, when probed too deeply are dropped and broken, shattered in a thousand slivers of silvery glass beyond reconstruction, when left alone, the truest friend, the source of a thousand whispered words, the collective memory of all past life, forgotten pain that returns again and again, the question on a test patiently waiting for a correct response, thoughts in artful forms, dreams that elevate a mind from gritty streets, the noise of grinding, grating mechanisms beneath the bus shifting gears, and amber lights above the driver indicating day and time, a decision to be made, to get off the bus, take the back way home down another hill, standing, waiting near the back door, then pulling the cord, the bus begins to stop and two feet away is another pale face, a darker coat, watching, desperate to say something, blank-faced and uncertain, he tells me to have a good day, as if he has a need to share these few words, as if blasting through an invisible wall he makes this effort, makes a human connection, sighs, has something to mention at the next meeting where he will introduce himself by his first name and claim success, what I respond to with caution, a nod of my head when I could have said something more, could have returned the gesture in a kinder way before leaving the bus with my book, the cold windy walk home and all the while, pursued by this thought, who are these people, from where did they come, and how is it on a winters day they appear in my life and speak to me when no one does this on a bus, on the sidewalk where strangers pass, when the most sacred rule is to avoid each other at an arm's-length silence, no acknowledgment of any kind, sitting single and alone with the pain on the bus, the hunger and afflictions, the eternal impossibility of making any significant contributions toward collective commercial potential, how is it on a dull gray afternoon they approach as if they know who I am, like those smiles in the grocery store aisle that seem in passing, amused if not interested, that offer the smallest bit of hope I am not alone — as they wish not to be — these small acts of courage, the opportunities I did not, would not accept, that I rushed away from, chased by fear and a danger about to plunder what little I still held together, wanting, planning a moment someday to smile in return the way so many have shared some kindness with me, to listen as someone speaks, shoot a meditational game of pool, sit in the quiet presence of another as we read books, looking up from time to time to share a thought, reflect on a past long gone and a distant future that might be, another day, some day, something to move toward… what, forgiveness, absolution, days in a life, the turning of a page, the small regret when the book must end, that blank empty space where a new one begins. (1989)

About the Authors

[The authors of this book are listed alphabetically by last names, with page references to their stories.]

Donna Anderson
DONNA ANDERSON joined the Tacoma (WA) Writer's Roundtable after the group published its first anthology in 2000. I thought maybe I could write well enough to get published, and it turns out I can. The editor of my manuscripts says my sentences tend to become paragraphs; so when I heard about the one-story sentences challenge, that was right down my alley. pp. 58, 76

Ruth Anderson
RUTH ANDERSON is a retired USAF intelligence officer and published author living in Washington State enjoying volunteering as an adult literacy tutor because "if we don't teach adults to read they won't buy this book to help with vocabulary and plot development and may persuade some to become authors, so they can contribute to the next edition..." pp. 94, 125

Judy Ashley
JUDY ASHLEY recently retired from a career in property management and now extends her writing to short stories and poems. She is a member of a creative writing group, performs with a local theater group, plays hand drums, and enjoys time with her grandchildren. She lives in Lakewood WA with her partner Ed. pp. 40, 113

Babz Clough
BABZ CLOUGH lives in the Boston MA area and has been a writer for as long as she can remember. She hopes to release her first novel in the coming year and currently works on a collection of short stories about grief and young widowhood. pp. 19, 28

Leslie Crane
LESLIE CRANE, a native of Seattle WA, lives north of the city in Shoreline. She worked as a 21-Dealer in Las Vegas, spent ten years in Property Management and ten years in banking before her current state of bliss: retirement. She now has time to travel and spend with friends, family, and pets. She makes jewelry, using her current passions — etching and riveting metals. p. 78

Debbie Davidson
DEBBIE DAVIDSON started writing when she was very young and had to wash dishes for the entire family. Because it seemed she'd never finish the task, she would entertain herself by creating stories. She notes, "This challenge, to tell a story in one sentence, was entertaining." pp. 42, 54

Susan de la Vergne
SUSAN DE LA VERGNE left the corporate ranks after 25 years in IT so she could to write. Today, she's a regular columnist for *IEEE Insight*, a career development publication for engineers, has been published in numerous print and online publications, and is author of four books. She lives in Los Angeles CA. p. 8

Val Dumond
VAL DUMOND, an incurable word-doodler, plays with words as if they were marbles, letting them roll where they will. Owner of Muddy Puddle Press in Lakewood WA, she edits books for other writers and often writes her own (the latest: *American-English*). She compiled the stories for this book. pp. 97, 121

Joanne Johnston Francis
JOANNE JOHNSTON FRANCIS writes in Tacoma WA, her adopted hometown. Her collection of short stories, *Dearest Sparrow & Other Stories of Altered Lives* is available on Amazon or at the Pacific Northwest Shop in Tacoma. Her six-part title story links many lives over a half century in a romance like no other. p. 56

Yazmin Grant
YAZMIN ESTEFANIA FORD was born in Panama City, Panama, and moved to the USA at the age of 23. She is a teacher, Spanish interpreter, and motivational speaker. She loves to write in journals as a personal style of praying. p. 64

Doris Hughes Green
DORIS HUGHES GREEN is founder and CEO of Divine Divas Ministries, LLC. She has published her autobiography, *The Reason Why*, and hosts the weekly New Beginnings radio show at KLAY1180.com. Her mission is to change the world by spreading the love of Jesus through partnering with other businesses and blessing each other forward. p. 72

JoAnn Lakin Jackson
JOANN LAKIN JACKSON retired after 37 years teaching in Steilacoom WA. At 82, she stays active with dog show activities and her award winning Irish Wolfhounds and Border Terrier, and writing. She is President of the Plateau Area Writers Association and is about to publish her most recent book, *Naughty Dog Tales (Tails.)* p. 60

Paul Jackson

PAUL JACKSON, a retired Special Librarian and Instructor of Research — an editor/writer, a chorister, timpanist, and jazz drummer — became interested in writing in college when he was paid for his final exam article. He has published books, articles, and essays that include his Carl Sandburg-like sentences. pp. 13, 14

Sara Jacobelli

SARA JACOBELLI has worked numerous jobs: dishwasher, bus girl, bartender, newspaper reporter, private investigator's assistant, special education teacher, and librarian. She lives in New Orleans LA and writes fiction and nonfiction, published in such places as *Drunk Monkeys Literary Magazine, Bartleby Snopes, First Stop Fiction, Fiction on the Web, The Story Shack, Page & Spine, Postcard Shorts, The New Laurel Review*, and *The New York Times Metropolitan Diary*. pp. 66, 82

Gordon Kenny

GORDON KENNY writes romantic novels of the historic kind from his home in southern Indiana. He plays banjo for fellow seniors at the residence where he lives and often takes part in community theater productions. He is currently working on a story about Daniel Boone for children. p. 85

Stanley Krippner

STANLEY KRIPPNER, PhD, a professor of psychology at Saybrook University at Oakland CA since 1972, was awarded the American Psychological Association Award for Distinguished Contributions to the International Advancement of Psychology for work conducting seminars and workshops around the world. He has authored a list of books as long as your arm, his most recent, *Sex and Love in the 21st Century: An Introduction to Sexology for Young People.* (2017). p. 34

Jane Lang

JANE LANG has taken many writing classes over the years at community colleges and says, "I have never had quite enough words for a novel, but plenty roll off my pen, and I am comfortable, with poetry." She attends a poetry class at her senior center and is a member of a critique group, Striped Water Poets. p. 9

Diane H. Larson

DIANE H. LARSON, author of the novel, *The Kingdom Beyond the Sunset*, and three stories published in the first *One-Sentence-Stories* anthology, is a retired psychotherapist who lives in Gig Harbor WA with her beloved husband Dwight (AKA "Himself"), and their small dog Bertie. She recently discovered a particular delight in writing true-to-life one-sentence-stories. pp. 20, 44, 70

> [EDITOR'S NOTE: Because Diane submitted three stories almost before the ink was dry on Book#1 and before rules for Book#2 were announced, all three appear in this edition.]

Jeff Laskowski

JEFF LASKOWSKI is a retired salesman who enjoys tennis, bicycling, and cooking. In his spare time, he likes to restore old motorcycles and bicycles, which he has six of each. He and his wife reside in the beautiful community of Gig Harbor WA. p. 6

Benjamin Lukoff

BENJAMIN LUKOFF'S interest in local history was kindled at age six, when his father bought him *Pig-Tail Days in Old Seattle*, by Sophie Frye Bass, granddaughter of the city founder, Arthur A. Denny, at the gift shop of the Seattle (WA) Museum of History and Industry. Benjamin is the author of *Seattle Then and Now* (Pavilion, 2015). p. 1

Kate McPhail

KATE MCPHAIL is the author of eight children's books, three poetry collections, and three non-fiction books available on Amazon. Kate is a retired teacher who enjoys gardening, swimming, and playing violin. She lives in beautiful Southern Oregon with her spoiled cats. Contact Kate at kay8mcp@gmail.com. p. 7

Michael Miller

MICHAEL MILLER, a grandson of Scottish Immigrants with family ties to Ireland, lives with his cats in Hylebos, WA, on Puget Sound. A retired professor of English, he writes short essays and stories to share his observations of life. p. 135

Joyce Moody

JOYCE MOODY, of Lakewood WA, carries paper and pencils with her and jots notes for her stories. She writes mostly daytimes at the library and feels committed to writing stories of the many animal friends that seem to live in her head. p. 62

Nick Page

NICK PAGE is a musician specializing in the choral arts. He has over one hundred published choral works, several of which he has conducted at Carnegie Hall. Nick is also known as a song leader, comfortable in all styles. His first love, though, has always been writing. www.nickmusic.com pp. 5, 32

Panjah Of Jesus

PANJAH OF JESUS abides in Washington State with her God-given husband and three children, finishing up her Masters in Divinity. Her latest book, *Fat Government: Political Musings by the Future President of the United States of America*, is faith-filled detailing why she believes God has called and chosen her to be President of the United States in nine years." pp. 11, 16

Nita Penfold

NITA PENFOLD is writer/artist digging deep for the taste of the grit and honey in everyday life, creating from the dark currents of the spirit. A graduate of Lesley University's Masters of Arts in Writing program, her poetry has been widely published in anthologies, most recently in *The Absence of Something Specified*, and in the *Charters & Charters* text book, *Literature & Its Writers* (5th edition). pp. 10, 17

Crystal Perryman

CRYSTAL QUETURA PERRYMAN, a native Panamanian and the first of her family born in the U.S., is Executive Producer of Divas Ministry LLC on the "New Beginnings" radio talk show (KLAY-AM1180, Sundays, 11a.m. PST/1p.m. EST), and the mother of pretty Urielle. On a Sunday afternoon, you'll find her just chilling with the Divine Divas. p. 109

Suezy Proctor

SUEZY PROCTOR is author of *Marching Orders for the Military Sales Professional*. Her essays have been published in *Stratus: Journal of Arts & Writing*, and *Chrysalis: Outer Castings* and *Emergence Memoir*, and in publications of the University of Washington. She is a Seattle native living in Northern Alabama with husband Dan, pets Zoi and Cleo, and a gazillion cicadas. pp. 22, 68, 74

> [EDITOR'S NOTE: Because Suezy submitted three stories almost before the ink was dry on Book#1 and before rules for Book#2 were announced, all three appear in this edition.]

Angela Richardson

ANGELA RICHARDSON, a transplanted Brit, is a talented writer of sci-fi books for young people and mystery stories for grownups — her latest, *Murder on Baringo Island*. She lives in her rural estate at the foot of the Smoky Mountains in Tennessee where she sings, dances, paints, raises laying hens, cares for her pet pugs, and writes. p. 48

Michael Robbins

MICHAEL ROBBINS experiments with odd ideas and bizarre artworks. His stories have appeared in three previous Muddy Puddle collections. The follow-up book to his *Butterfly & Serpent* series is in progress. He lives in the Pacific Northwest with his wife of 22 years, Roberta. p. 50

Nick Romeo

NICK ROMEO is a multidisciplinary artist, musician, and writer with work published in such literary magazines as: *StreetCake Magazine, Uppagus, Nowhere Journal, Eye Contact, Moonshine Review*. He was interviewed for "Pankhearst's Fresh Featured", "The Dailey Poet Site", and *Southern Florida Poetry Journal*, and received press on *featuredpoet.com*. Nick lives with his wife and their cat Megatron in Pittsburgh PA. pp. 52, 100

Terry Sager

TERRY SAGER writes psychological thrillers, exploring the dark side of the human psyche. She is a member of the Pacific Northwest Writers Association. The rainy Pacific Northwest, where Terry lives, is often the setting of her sinister plots. When not writing, she is a volunteer at the local humane society and is an advocate for animal welfare. pp. 106, 117

Jennifer Schneider

JENNIFER SCHNEIDER is a life-long learner, online educator, and book lover committed to ensuring all students of opportunities to achieve their educational goals. She practices, learns, and instructs in the legal, business, and humanities disciplines. Based in Pennsylvania, she enjoys writing in public libraries and coffee shops up and down the East Coast. pp. 24, 30

Jessica Schulz

JESSICA SCHULZ recently relocated from California to Alabama and is adjusting to a new lifestyle and locale. Our book club leader suggested that we try our hands at writing one-sentence stories. I had a lot of fun "rejecting Teacher's advice" and letting myself run on-and-on! p. 26

Richard Silverman

RICHARD SILVERMAN has been writing seriously (but not ambitiously) since his mid-30s, ever since he discovered that thinking and word-crafting are what satisfy him most. He's worked as a freelance commercial writer and has been published a few times. But he's an "artist" by nature who writes mostly for himself and for online readers who welcome his expressed print. He says, "My writing soothes my soul." pp. 2, 3

Billie A. Stewart

BILLIE STEWART lives in Lakewood, WA, attends the Lakewood Senior Center where she writes her memoirs. She raised four daughters after being widowed at 35 and went back to college for a Master's Degree in Social Work. She loves to travel and has lived, worked, and played abroad for many years. p. 130

Jim Teeters

JIM TEETERS, MSW, writes books on teaching and learning, poetry collections, and an eBook novel with his grandson. He volunteers as a poetry facilitator and is active in the Striped Water Poets group. Jim is a retired social worker living in Kent WA. His latest book is *Because of This: Lao Tzu's Tao Te Ching (Barclay Press, 2018)*. p. 88

Geoffrey Williams
GEOFFREY WILLIAMS is Professor of Applied Linguistics at a French University. He is a lexicographer, past president of EURALEX, and perpetual dreamer. He has never been on a boat for longer than an English Channel crossing, and no one in their right mind would let him drive one. p. 38

Kathy Wilson
KATHY WILSON has enjoyed a variety of life experiences as bartender, motel maid, clam digger, logger, construction superintendent, roofing contractor, realtor, landscaper, Certified Professional Coach, website designer snowmobile clothing manufacturer, Tai Chi instructor, and author. For more about Kathy, visit www.Warrior-Priestess.com/ p. 91

Marsha Willsey
MARSHA WILLSEY was born in Tennessee, raised in Michigan, and has returned to the south in Madison AL, where she writes her stories and is a member of Books in Review. Now retired, she and her Yankee husband of 45 years have two children and three grandchildren. p. 15

Carol Wissmann
CAROL WISSMANN is a former freelance writer for more than 70 publications, a college writing tutor, and presenter of her "Profiting from Periodicals" workshop at colleges and writers conferences. She now works as an author publicist and can be reached at CRWissmann@gmail.com/ p. 12

Anne Wood
ANNE WOOD, Adult Services Librarian at the Madison (AL) Public Library, is the proud mother of two rescued fur-children, Randy and Evie. She also fosters homeless dogs through *A New Leash on Life*. Anne is a vegetarian, enjoys yoga, wine, the Rolling Stones, and stories of all kinds as co-facilitator of a reading group called Books in Review. p. 46

hollie woodie

HOLLY WOODIE was born and raised in new orleans and lived in new york city for nine years before moving back home. She writes because she must and has written for as long as she can remember. hollie has been published in *The New Laurel Review* and the *New Orleans Avant Garde*. pp. 4, 80

Barbara Wyatt

BARBARA WYATT writes for many magazines including *Northwest Travel, Good Old Boat, American Style, Boys' Life,* and *New York Tennis Magazine*. Her new book, *Ode to Tennis* (2017), is a humorous rhyming poem about a recreational player's effort to learn the game of tennis. p. 103

Made in the USA
Lexington, KY
17 April 2018